Outrageous Love

Outrageous Love

A Story of Covenant Faithfulness

Wes Feltner, Ph.D.

Outrageous Love
A Story of Covenant Faithfulness
Copyright©2024 by Wes Feltner, Ph.D

Critical Mass Books
Haymarket, Virginia
www.criticalmasspublishing.com

1st Edition

ISBN: 978-1-947153-49-3

Cover Design   Eowyn Riggins
Interior Layout   Rachel Newhouse

One

An Unexpected Discovery

Jill liked to keep things on schedule, and it was Monday, so that meant one thing—laundry. Lots of it. The washer and dryer were in the basement, and she had already made three trips down the stairs by the time she got to the basket with her husband's clothes.

As she sorted them, she thought about the nice quiet weekend—at least, as quiet as things could be with three kids, football on the tube, and the dog barking during a thunderstorm that raced through the area on Sunday. Quiet? Sure. It was a protracted period of domestic bliss. The chaos was delightful and calming.

She savored every moment.

Tom had been gone all week, coming through the door late Friday afternoon. His work as a sales rep took him to so many conferences in sometimes faraway places. This time it was Vegas. He had asked her to go with him, but she had gone there with him before and hated the place. The heat. The atmosphere. All of it. She wasn't a prude—not at all—but there was something about that place that seemed, well, just dirty. Tom told her he felt the same way, too. He had been dreading the trip, calling home several times a day just to tell Jill he missed her. He was good like that.

That's why what happened next hit her like a ton of bricks.

As she sorted Tom's clothes for the wash, an ordinary looking business card fell out of his khaki's pocket. She almost didn't look at it, but then thought maybe it was something he needed. She picked it up from the floor and turned it over. It took her a moment to focus because she'd left her reading glasses upstairs, but she could make out the word "escorts."

After she raced upstairs to read the details, sure enough, it was a business card for a prostitute service. Jill sat down on a chair at the kitchen table. Her mind was spinning. So was the room. Why did Tom have such a thing in his pocket? Then she recalled how the sidewalks in Vegas were littered with cards about all kinds of "services." *That must be it*, she thought. *But why was it in his pocket? Maybe a prank by one of his buddies?*

Just as she was about to dismiss it and give her husband the benefit of the doubt, she turned it over and saw something that wasn't visible when she picked up the card from the basement floor—what with the dim light and no reading glasses. There was a personal note written on it.

A name and phone number.

She looked over at the clock on the wall. Tom wouldn't be home for at least six hours. She thought about calling him at the office but decided to simply wait for a face-to-face talk that evening.

The day seemed to drag by, and by the time he got home, the kids were there. So, she put on a cheerful front through dinner and homework, opting to wait until the kids were in bed to show him what she'd found. Finally, the time was right. Tom was brushing his teeth in the bathroom of their room. She walked in and placed the card on the sink counter.

Their eyes met in the mirror.

"What's this?" she asked, after a moment of awkward silence.

He looked at the card and said, "Um, it's nothing." Then, after another pause, "I don't want to talk about it."

"You don't want to talk about it? We *have* to talk about it!"

"Why?"

She shifted back onto her heels, her hands spread in disbelief. "Because this card is for a prostitute. Did you sleep with her?"

He spat into the sink and rinsed his mouth. Looking down at his toothbrush while he rinsed it under the faucet he said, "You know I would never do anything like that."

She waited silently until he'd put his toothbrush carefully away. "Look at me, Tom. Give me a straight answer. Did you?

His eyes told her before his voice. "Yes."

An Unexpected Surprise

It was finally noon on Friday. Unbeknownst to his wife, Nick had taken the afternoon off to surprise her with a mind-blowing, romantic extravaganza. He'd been waiting for this day for weeks and had to concentrate to keep from speeding on the way home. He hoped he hadn't forgotten anything, but he was pretty sure he'd covered all logistics. Few people would call him a romantic type, but today was a milestone wedding anniversary after a tough year and he'd really thrown his heart into making it memorable.

He'd consulted Google about couples deals and venues, had checked and double-checked availability and reservations, and had even clocked the time required to get from place to place to be sure that it would go without a hitch. It was going to be spectacular. He was going to show up with flowers from Bachman's and a box from Nordstrom's. They'd check into the Graves Hotel, where he had a spa package all planned out for her, complete with hair and makeup. Relaxed and beautified, they'd go up to their room and she'd open the Nordstrom's box to find the fancy dress that his sister had helped him to select for her (with shoes!), and they'd both get dressed to the nines.

Then a limo would pick them up at the door for the trip to the Butcher and the Boar for dinner before taking them to the State Theater for a show that she'd been longing to see. Then, the luxurious drive back to the hotel where their night would eventually end with a glass of red wine. It was going to be the best anniversary they'd ever had.

He was grinning from ear to ear in anticipation when he pulled into the driveway next to a car that didn't look familiar. He snatched up the flowers and box, hoping the unknown visitor wouldn't put a wrench in his grand plans. When he stepped through the garage door into the house, he was surprised to hear strange noises upstairs. With growing anxiety, he climbed the stairs and walked to their bedroom door. When it swung open, his wife and another man frantically grabbed at their clothes while he stood frozen in shock.

Stop the camera in your mind and answer the following question; if you were in Jill's place or in Nick's place, how would *you* respond? Would you throw your arms up in the air and shout? Would you burst into tears? Would you throw a lamp – or a punch? Would you deny what you were seeing? Would you turn and walk silently away? Would you do all of the above? Take your time and think, or perhaps you knew before I asked. Now write your response down; you'll want it in a minute. What would you do if you were Jill/Nick in that situation? Now, with that response written down, let me tell you how Jill and Nick actually responded.

An Unexpected Response

After Jill's husband admitted to being with a Las Vegas prostitute, Jill took a deep breath and said, "Tom, I want you to take tomorrow off work, and I want you to cancel all of your appointments because we are going to spend all day together and I'm going to romance you like you can't imagine."

And Nick? Well, Nick stood in the doorway of his bedroom, arms full of lilies, staring down the man climbing out of *his* bed. "Leave, and don't even *think* about coming back here." Then Nick stepped out of the doorway, toward his wife, so that the man could scoot out the door and go quickly away. They stood silently, looking at each other as the man's footsteps faded toward the front door. Nick then said, "Honey, put some clothes on while I put these flowers in a vase. We're about to experience the best anniversary we've ever had."

Now, look at the response that you wrote down. Does it resemble, in any way, the response of Jill or Nick? Of course it doesn't. No human on earth would respond in that way to either one of those situations. It's shocking to even *think* that anyone would respond like that. Nor should they, that's not right. That's insane. Exactly.

Did you know there is a love like that?

James 4:4 says that you and I have prostituted ourselves with worldly lovers. Yet God, according to His boundless love in Jesus Christ, wines and dines us anyway. That's the scandal of the gospel. It's shocking. It's outrageous. It's a scandal beyond all scandals. And it's what the book of Hosea is all about: The outrageous, insane, unthinkable love of God towards those who have brazenly and wantonly given their love to things other than God. That is the immeasurable, limitless love that is revealed in the story of Hosea.

The story of Hosea helps us *feel* God's love

For most of us, the love of God is head knowledge. We know God is a loving God. We know that He loves us individually. We have read, "*God is love*," in I John 4. We have sung, *Jesus loves me, this I know,* since we were little children, but do we *feel* it? Do we emotionally feel it gripping us? Hosea helps us to feel God's love by using powerful language in metaphor, in symbolism that we can identify with. The language gets you emotionally involved; it is intended to grip you emotionally so that you feel the love of God.

The story of Hosea helps us understand our unfaithfulness

Not only does Hosea help us feel God's love, but it helps us understand sin. When you and I think about sin, we often tend to think of the *fruit* rather than the *root* of what sin is. Here's what I mean. Take lying, for example. We tend to think that the issue is the lie, but the issue really is not the lie. It is the love underneath. The problem is not that we are liars, the problem is that we are lovers.

Let me explain. The lie is the fruit of the sin, the result, the manifestation. The reason we lie is because we love acceptance. That is the root. We are loving something like reputation, or the approval of someone, or to get some advantage – some type of god of acceptance. And my love for that is the reason I lie, to get that acceptance or approval, or to keep it. See, the issue is not the lie. It is the love of something other than God.

This is important. If the number one command, as Jesus said, is to love God with all your heart, then the number one sin is loving things *other than God* with all your heart. That is the fundamental root issue with sin. It is not the thing itself, but the love of something other than God that is at the core of that behavior. If I love the god of acceptance, then I lie as an act of worship to my god. The book of Hosea helps to expose those idols of the heart. It helps us do the hard work of uncovering what it is that we really love. What is the idol or the false god that my heart is chasing?

The story of Hosea helps us grow in the gospel

Not only does Hosea help you feel God's love and help you understand what sin is, it also helps us grow in the gospel. The story of Hosea is an Old Testament picture of the love of Christ that is seen in the gospel. Let me put it this way, if you think marrying a prostitute is a scandal, just wait till you get to the cross. If marrying a prostitute is outrageous, imagine dying for one. That is what Hosea prepares us for as we come to the gospel in the New Testament. Hosea helps us to understand the gospel of Jesus Christ. So, let's dive in.

Two

The three main themes of this minor prophet are all found in chapter one. Hosea's first theme deals very plainly with *a wayward people*. Now, we don't know a lot about Hosea. We know that he is likely from the northern kingdom. If you remember, when King Solomon died, the kingdom of Israel split into two different kingdoms: The northern kingdom, Israel, and the southern kingdom, Judah, which also included the tribe of Benjamin.

Generally speaking, the kings in the northern kingdom were a lot more wicked than the kings in the southern kingdom. And if you look at the names of the kings listed in verse one, we can conclude that Hosea ministered to the Kingdom of Israel in the eighth century, roughly 750 BC. The counterparts or colleagues of Hosea would be the prophets Isaiah, Amos, and Micah, and the reason that is important is because it leads us to the next understanding. If

Hosea was a prophet during that time, that means he was ministering during a time of economic prosperity.

You see, under Isaiah and Jeroboam II the nation experienced what you might call a second golden age, the first one, of course, being the time of King David. This was a second golden age. It is true that Assyria was on the rise, but Israel and Judah, the northern and southern kingdoms, were not quite feeling the pressure of that yet. So, they were partying like it's 1999. Things were booming economically, the borders were expanding along with their horizons, and they were living it up. This was a very prosperous time in the nation of Israel and in Judah.

Why does that matter? Knowing when Hosea was ministering, and the prosperity of that time, helps us understand the trend of the kingdoms and what they were struggling with, namely, a moral decline and idolatry. Prosperity often breeds idolatry, both then and now. Here's why: It is easy to fall in love with money if you have lots of it. That is why Jesus said it is hard for a rich man to get into the kingdom of God, because his heart begins to love money (or the things money can provide) instead of God.

As often happens in periods of moral decline, the abuse of power was common. The powerful took advantage of the poor, and there was drunkenness, theft, and murder. And it didn't help matters when King Ahab married an Assyrian princess, Jezebel, who brought her Assyrian gods, Baal and Ishhara (or Ishtar), with her. I Kings 16 says that, *"Ahab, son of Omri did more evil in the eyes of the Lord than any of those before him."* Ahab built a temple in Samaria, and he, himself, set up the altar for Baal in it, as well as making an Ishhara pole.

So, the people of Israel were worshiping idols and they were crediting all of their prosperity not to the generous hand of God – but to their false gods.

So, knowing when Hosea ministered helps us understand the economic prosperity of the time, which helps us understand the idolatry that was sweeping the land, which brings us to the metaphor. The context sets the stage for the main metaphor in the book of Hosea, namely, Israel's sin is illustrated by the relationship between Hosea and Gomer. Let's look at it. *"When the Lord first spoke through Hosea, the Lord said to him, 'Go, take for yourself a wife of whoredom and have children of whoredom, for the land commits great whoredom by forsaking the Lord.'"* Hosea 1:2.

"And the Lord said to me, 'Go again, love a woman who is loved by another man and is an adulteress, even as the Lord loves the children of Israel, though they turn to other gods....'" Hosea 3:1. This was a real relationship between real people, Hosea and Gomer, a real-life metaphor of a faithful God married to a wayward people – a living example of Israel and her unfaithfulness to God.

Because marriage is the metaphor, the book of Hosea contains language that we might consider PG13, rated R, or even X rated. It speaks of prostitution, adultery, and whoring because it is playing off the metaphor of marriage. And this is not new imagery in the scripture. The scripture uses this kind of language often. Let me give you two examples. Ezekiel 6:9 says, *"Then those of you who escape will remember me among the nations where they are carried captive, how I have been broken over their whoring heart that has departed from me and over their eyes that go whoring after their idols."*

And James 4:4, *"You adulterous people! Do you not know that friendship with the world is enmity with God? Therefore, whoever wishes to be a friend of the world makes himself an enemy of God."* Do you love God or do you love the world? The imagery, the metaphor that is used is that of an adulterous people, and this was not a random choice of metaphor.

Adultery, prostitution, betrayal, unfaithfulness, whoring – these words echo deeply in the human psyche. Perhaps not even murder gets a stronger response, this is so personal, so intimate a rejection. The language used in the book of Hosea is used frequently in scripture as a metaphor for our sin. It is the image that best demonstrates to us how extreme the offense of idolatry is to God. I said earlier that Hosea helps us to feel God's love for us. By using the metaphor of marriage to an adulterous partner, Hosea also helps us to feel what *God* feels when we are unfaithful to Him. This is an anguish that any human can understand and feel, even if only in imagination.

It is not just the sin of adultery, itself. To God, sin is sin. Adultery is a sin like lying, gluttony, murder, coveting, pride, theft. So why is this spiritual adultery or spiritual idolatry such a big deal? This is important – it is not because the sin itself is a big deal. It is that *God* is a big deal.

God is *the* big deal.

Here is what I mean. Staying within the metaphor of marriage, God is the best, most satisfying, treat-you-the-way-you-ought-to-be-treated, gorgeous, rich, strong, sensitive, faithful, thoughtful, loving husband you could ever ask for. God is everything the heart longs for. This is why it is a big deal when your heart longs for something else. It is not the sin itself that is such a big deal. It is the fact that you're running to some punk kid rather than experiencing the love of a real man. That is the imagery we get here.

C.S. Lewis put it this way in *The Weight of Glory*, he said, "Our Lord finds our desires not too strong, but too weak. We are half-hearted creatures, fooling about with drink and sex and ambition when infinite joy is offered us, like an ignorant child who wants to go on making mud pies in a slum because he cannot imagine what is meant by the offer of a holiday at the sea. We are far too easily pleased."

To bring that back into Hosea's metaphor, we settle for "punks," that is, we settle for the idols of the world (money, sex, fame, security) because we cannot imagine what it would be like to be loved by a real man. God is everything your heart was created to long for. You and I have pushed past our glorious One True Love and trotted down to the pimps on the corner to satisfy our deepest longings.

"A Warning of Judgment"

The second main theme is found in Hosea 1:4. *"And the Lord said to him, call his name Jezreel for in just a little while, I will punish the house of Jehu for the blood of Jezreel, and I will put an end to the kingdom of the house of Israel. And on that day, I will break the bow of Israel in the valley of Jezreel."* An accounting is coming.

In the ancient near east, names represented realities in a way that they do not in our time. These days, people give their kid a name because they think it's cool, or because it was their Grandparent's name, or they read it in a baby book and liked it. But back then, names had meaning and often that meaning represented reality. Now, if I named my son Jezreel, that probably would not mean anything to you unless you are an Old Testament scholar. But if I named my child Benedict Arnold...well, that would carry some meaning. Or the name Nixon or Manson, those names are loaded with associations.

To the Jews in the ancient near east, Jezreel was a valley where many battles took place. It was known to be a place of bloodshed. So, naming your child Jezreel would be like naming him Armageddon. The mind immediately flinches. You think, *Yikes, that's a bad thing. That is a judgment. That is bloodshed and war.*

That is the point.

Hosea marries Gomer, a whore, to model Israel's condition as a wayward people. Then Hosea issues God's warning of judgment to come for Israel's whoring after other gods by naming their first child Jezreel, a place of bloody judgment (which happened in 722 BC when Assyria rose to its full power and crushed the northern Kingdom, Israel). That seems clear enough, but the message was not complete.

Hosea 1:6-10, "*She conceived again and bore a daughter. And the Lord said to him, 'Call her name No Mercy* [Loruhamah], *for I will no more have mercy on the house of Israel, to forgive them at all. But I will have mercy on the house of Judah and I will save them by the Lord their God. I will not save them by bow or sword or by war or by horses or by horsemen.*'

When she had weaned No Mercy, she conceived and bare a son. Then God said, 'Call his name Not My People [Loammi]: *for you are not my people and I will not be your God.'"*

Wow. There is not a lot of wiggle room for interpretation in that message. And I want to point out something about this message from God. We live in an age of 24-hour news cycles and instant messaging. We can bounce a message off a satellite in space to someone on the other side of the Earth in seconds. And we like our stories in 45-minute units (plus commercial breaks). God doesn't work on our timetable. It took Gomer nine months to make a baby back then just like it takes women today, and they nursed longer. (They didn't have Gerber's or Evenflo at the local market.) So, conception to weaning took roughly three years. God warned His people more and more pointedly over a period of about a decade. That doesn't change the meaning of the message in any way. It is just good to be reminded of the realities while reading short stories in the Bible. Hosea's message wasn't two or three sermons and a subtle naming puzzle. God gave Israel plenty of clear warning for a long time. Very easy to overlook in a short story.

Now let's pull the full message together. First there was the main theme of a wayward people seen in the relationship of Hosea and Gomer. That intimate relationship also describes the scope of the message: This is a family affair between God and *His* people. This is emphasized when He exempts His people of Judah, the Southern Kingdom. And God uses Hosea's and Gomer's children to present the warning of judgment that is the second theme. What is His warning? Jezreel, a place of bloodshed. Loruhamah, No Mercy. Loammi, Not My People. The judgment that was coming would be bloody and merciless, and would be a repudiation of the Northern Kingdom as God's people. God was going to *disown* Israel. That was the judgment that was prophesied by Hosea to the people of Israel. They would be cast out of God's family.

And isn't that the proper response? Isn't that what you do with whores? Expose them, shame them, shun them. Send them away. Have nothing more to do with them. Expunge their names. Isn't that how it is supposed to end? The sinner gets judgment and that is the end of the story.

"The Wooing of God"

That is not the end of God's story. That is nowhere close to the end of the story. There is a third, glorious, theme in the book of Hosea. The first was of a wayward people, the second gave warning of judgment to come, but the third isn't their obvious destruction at the hands of the Assyrians. The third theme begins, and is revealed in, the first word of Hosea 1:10, "*Yet.*" Praise God for the little word, *yet*, also known as *but, nevertheless,* and *however.* It is one of the greatest words in all of the Bible. Aren't you eternally grateful for the word *yet?* *Yet,* to the sinner, is great news. *Yet,* to those who are rightfully condemned, is wonderful news. Let me give you two examples elsewhere in scripture of the good news of *yet.*

In Jonah 2:5, when Jonah is experiencing judgment from God in the deep water, in the belly of the great fish, he gives a vivid description of his situation. He says, "*The waters closed in over me to take my life; the deep surrounded me; weeds were wrapped about my head at the roots of the mountains. I went down to the land whose bars closed upon me forever;* **Yet** *you brought up my life from the pit, oh Lord my God."* Praise God for *yet.* "I deserved judgment, *yet* you brought me up."

Let me give you another example in the New Testament. Ephesians 2:3, *"Among whom we all once lived in the passions of our flesh, carrying out the desires of the body and the mind. We were by nature children of wrath just like the rest of mankind.* **But** *God being rich in mercy because of the love with which he loved us...."* Praise God for *yet, but, nevertheless, and however.*

Here is the divine plot twist at the end of God's story. Israel is a wayward people, symbolized by Hosea and Gomer. Judgment is coming upon them, symbolized by their three children. We look forward, expecting to see the deserved obliteration and rejection of Israel and we see this. *"Yet the number of the children of Israel shall be like the sand of the sea, which cannot be measured or numbered. And in the place where it is said to them, you are not my people, there it shall be said to them, you are the children of the living God. And the children of Judah and the children of Israel shall be gathered together and they shall appoint for themselves one head, and they shall come up out of the land: for great shall be the day of Jezreel."*

Here is the good news of yet, "My people are wayward and they are deserving of judgment, *yet* I will bless them, their number will be as the sands of the sea. Though they are unfaithful to me, I will not break the promise I made to Abraham, *I* will be faithful to *them.* They shall reap what they have sowed, they will be scattered, *but* they will be restored. They are going to be brought back from not-my-people to Children of the Living God."

When it comes to the love of God, there is no such thing as a point of no return. The fire of God's love cannot be put out by the waterfall of your sin.

That is the good news of the book of Hosea. As we sing often in the praise song, "Our sins, they are many, His mercy is more." If this feels like a scandal to you, if this feels outrageous to you, then you are probably starting to understand the love of God. If you grew up singing *Jesus loves me, this I know* and you're moving toward *Amazing Love, How Can It Be,* now you're getting it. You're beginning to get a feeling of how boundless God's love is.

But you may be thinking, why would God do this? Why would God love "whores" this way? Why would God, when He can have a princess, choose a prostitute? Here's why. Hosea 11:8. *"How can I give you up, Ephraim [which is Israel, the Northern Kingdom]? How can I hand you over, Israel? How can I make you like Admah? How can I treat you like Zeboim?* [Admah and Zeboim were destroyed with Sodom and Gomorrah.] *My heart recoils within me. My compassion grows warm and tender. I will not execute my burning anger. I will not again destroy Ephraim: for I am God, not a man, the Holy One in your midst and I will not come in wrath."*

There it is, right there. Why does God do this? Why does God love so boundlessly? Why does God love so insanely? Is it because he takes pity on you? No. It is just who He is. It is just *what* He is. He IS love, (I John 4:8) Did you see the "for," the reason why He would not destroy? *"For I am God, not a man."* I love like this because I am God, I am love. My love is grounded in Me.

God's love does not depend on how good you are. It doesn't depend on how lovable you are. He doesn't consider whether you deserve to be loved this way. If that were the case, we would not be loved. God loves because He IS love, and He is boundless, and it is His nature to love in a boundless way. The love of God is grounded in God, not in your goodness. That is the best news in the world, for God is unchanging.

So how should we respond to this love of God? How should we feel about His willingness to love and bless those who are so undeserving? Well, first, you should feel shocked, totally shocked. Do you remember the song, *Amazing Love, How Can it Be?* That should be your first response. Astounded. Dumbfounded. How can it be true? And then, you should be thrilled, *thrilled*. Not only am I shocked that God loves me, but I am also *thrilled* that He loves me. Why? Because it is true. Because it is real. The love of God may be hard to believe, but it is not make-believe.

And then, we ought to be changed by this. This love changes everything. It changes how we see ourselves, how we can love ourselves. And it changes how we see others. When somebody starts to cast judgment on someone, Oh, look at them, they're a prostitute. Look at them, they're a drunk, they're an addict, they're – whatever – that is precisely the kind of person God loves. What the world calls an outcast, God takes ballroom dancing! So who are we to cast judgment on them when they are the very type of person the love of God pursues? And how do you know that? Because he did so for you!

So, in the first chapter of Hosea we have seen three main themes: A wayward people, the warning of judgment, and the wooing of God. We have seen how God's love is *yet, but, nevertheless, however*. We have seen how it keeps pursuing the wayward spouse, namely, you and me. And this is the very thing we see in the gospel of Jesus Christ. Do you remember the story? It was a Friday afternoon, and he wasn't what you would call the romantic type, but it was their anniversary, or, as they called it back then, Passover. And oh, how He wanted to celebrate this anniversary with his collective bride. He wanted to celebrate the day that He purchased Israel from the pimp known as Pharaoh. He wanted to celebrate the day when He entered into a marriage covenant with them at Mount Sinai. But when He arrived on Earth to pick them up, He found them chasing other lovers.

There was only one proper response. There was only one just way to deal with a whore like that: Judgment. Except His judgment was more scandalous than the sin itself. Why? Because the one who was judged was not the wayward wife. It was the faithful husband. And just as Hosea said, the judgment would be bloody, the judgment would show no mercy, and the judgment would treat The Son like He was Not My People. And yet that faithful husband so loved the world, He willingly took the judgment she deserved with joy.

And three days later, He prepared for her a table where He would wine and dine her for the rest of her eternal life. That – THAT – is the love God has for you in Christ Jesus.

Three

Everybody loves a good story

Her name is Scheherazade. She is one of the main characters from the folktale *One Thousand and One Nights*. The story is about a Persian king who discovers his wife has been unfaithful. In a fit of rage, he orders her execution. Even with his wife's death, the king's vengeance is not satisfied; it only intensifies. The king puts together a plan to rid the kingdom of all women; *he will marry a different woman every night, enjoy her for the evening, and have her killed in the morning.*

This goes on for days until he meets Scheherazade, the daughter of a court official. Scheherazade agrees to marry the king but has a plan. After the wedding, they go into the king's chambers and Scheherazade offers to tell the king a story. As it turns out, the story is so captivating that the king listens until the morning. But, Scheherazade refuses to tell the ending. The king keeps her alive another day as he *must* hear how the story ends. The next night she continues the story, which leads to another story more captivating than the first. That story leads to another, and this goes on for 1001 nights. By then, the king is so in love with Scheherazade that he spares her life.

Your initial thought might be, "**What an idiot!**" How could someone be so dumb? I mean, "*I'd never fall for something like that*." Unless, of course, the story was… *Yellowstone, The Walking Dead, Band of Brothers, Downton Abby, Friends, Game of Thrones, The Notebook*, or hands-down the all-time greatest, *The Godfather* (and all God's people said, "Amen."). Regardless of the series, the book, or the film, we all know what it is like to think, feel, or say, "One more episode." You see, we are not unlike the king, we are captivated by good stories. *It's why we go to movies, read novels, tell campfire stories, read to our children at bedtime!*

But stories not only captivate us; they can confront us in ways other genres cannot. For example, I could say, "Love your neighbor," or I could tell you a story that goes like this, "There was a man going down from Jerusalem who fell among robbers," the story of the Good Samaritan. I could say, "God forgives," or I could tell you a story that starts with, "A father had two sons," the story of the Prodigal Son. A good story confronts because it forces you to think about your life. If you think about it, you'll realize that metaphor is built into almost every communication in our lives. We experience it in so many different ways. Music could hardly exist without metaphor. Neither could poetry. Imagine a commercial without it. We use it in our own conversations. For example, I could talk about my inner struggles or my battles with anxiety, or I could paint it, like Edvard Munch did. I could say I love someone, or I could murmur, "What light through yonder window breaks? It is the east and Juliet is the sun." Or I could say, "I'm addicted to you," or I could play you a song, like *Tennessee Whiskey*. Those metaphors express the feelings we want to share, feelings that we want another person to understand.

That is what the story of Hosea is meant to do.

Metaphor has the power to drive a truth home.

The three-fold theme in Hosea is not just a good storytelling form. Each of those themes has a very real point. The living metaphor of faithful Hosea and his wayward wife is a relatable picture meant to elicit all of the feelings of outrage, agony, and betrayal that God feels because of the unfaithfulness of His people. The metaphors in the names of Hosea's children are not a threat – they are a warning of imminent judgment, both in the near future at the hands of the Assyrians, and the more significant judgment to come. And the third theme, God's boundless love revealed in His promise to make them His People again, a redemption effected by God Himself in the person of His Son becoming the Great Metaphor of our sin and bearing our judgment Himself – it doesn't get any more personal, or more loving, than that.

I could tell you that God loves you and you might agree with that. You might know that intellectually. You might even be able to quote John 3:16; but do you *feel* it? However, if I told you instead that God's love for you is like a man named Hosea who was married to a woman named Gomer, and Gomer was not only unfaithful, but she was a prostitute with many lovers. And not only was she a prostitute with many lovers, she had multiple children with those many lovers, and in light of all of her unfaithfulness, in light of everything she did to her faithful husband, her husband responded to her like this:

"Yet the number of the children of Israel shall be like the sand of the sea which cannot be measured or numbered. And in the place where it is said to them, 'You are not my people,' it shall be said to them, 'Children of the living God.' And the children of Judah and the children of Israel shall be gathered together and they shall appoint for themselves one head and they shall go up from the land. For great shall be the day of Jezreel. Say to your brothers, 'You are my people,' and to your sisters, 'You have received mercy.'" [Hosea 1:10-2:1)

That is outrageous. That is insane. Nobody loves that way. And yet, that is how God has loved you in the person of Jesus Christ. That metaphor, that imagery of faithfulness and unfaithfulness and all that the book of Hosea is stirring up in our minds, is to reveal to us the unfathomable love of God.

So, let's continue with the metaphor in Hosea. *"Plead with your mother, plead, for she is not my wife,* [That is, she is not acting like my wife] *and I'm not her husband, that she put away her whoring from her face, her adultery from between her breasts, lest I strip her naked and make her as in the day she was born, and make her like a wilderness, like a parched land, and kill her with thirst. Upon her children, also, I will have no mercy because they are children of whoredom, for their mother has played the whore. She who conceived them has acted shamefully. She said, I will go after my lovers who give me bread and water, and wool and flax, and oil and drink."*

This is a metaphor, a symbol, of spiritual adultery. The issue here is not actual adultery. The issue is idolatry. Adultery is simply the metaphor to describe the sin of idolatry. That is what's happening. And this imagery of marriage and unfaithfulness is used to describe the relationship between Israel and her faithful husband, God. The Bible describes our relationship with God as that of a covenant or a marriage. That is when you became a Christian. If you are a Christian, you looked to God and said, *I do.* That is what you did. You made a covenant with Him; you made a marriage-like commitment to God. You did not say, I promise I'll become a better person, or I promise I'll clean up my act or I promise I'll turn over a new leaf.

That is not what you said. If you are a Christian, what you said was, "God, I love you more than anything or anyone else in the world." That is what it means to be a Christian, and that is what Israel did when she entered into a marriage covenant with God. The record of it is in Exodus 19:7 where God spoke to Moses on Mount Sinai and offered to make a covenant with the descendants of Jacob (Israel). God said if they would obey Him fully and keep His covenant, then out of all of the nations, they would be His treasured possession. Then He sent Moses down to get Israel's answer.

"So Moses went back and summoned the elders of the people and set before them all these words that the Lord had commanded him to speak. And the people all responded together and said, 'All that the Lord has spoken, we will do.'" Have you ever heard that kind of language before? Have you ever been at a wedding ceremony where a spouse-to-be said "I do" to the other person? Well, that is

what Israel did. She heard God's offer, she considered the things that God was asking of her, and she said, "I do." It was a marriage covenant, and that is why, throughout the scripture, that metaphor, that imagery continues.

For instance, Isaiah 54:5 says, *"For your maker is your husband – the Lord Almighty is his name – and the Holy One of Israel is your Redeemer; the God of the whole earth, he is called. For the Lord has called you like a wife, deserted and grieved in spirit like a wife of youth when she is cast off, says your God."* So the language in the Old Testament referred to Israel as in a marriage with God; and that language carried over into the New Testament. Ephesians 5 talks about husbands and wives, giving a picture of Christ and His bride, the Church. And Revelation 19:7 says this, "Let us rejoice and exalt and give him the glory for the marriage of the Lamb has come and his bride has made herself ready."

The marriage metaphor used throughout the book of Hosea is this: When you enter into relationship with God, it is a covenant. It is like a marriage relationship where you say, "God, I love you more than anything or anyone else." This is of prime importance to God. It is why God's very first commandment in His covenant was, "You shall have no other gods before me." And Jesus reiterated its importance when He summed up the New Covenant as, *"You shall love the Lord your God with all your heart, and with all your soul, and with all your mind, and with all your strength."*

The Covenant that God made with Israel was like a marriage. He would be their God, and they would be His people, all they had to do was to love Him and be faithful to Him. The commandments He required of them were all for their good – love Him with their whole hearts, and love their neighbors as they loved themselves. In return, He would love them and be their God, and He would pour His grace on them.

Four

God gave His people plenty of instructions for how to treat one another, which was summed up in Leviticus 19:18 as "Love your neighbor as yourself." But He also gave them a plethora of other instructions that seem nonsensical to us today, things like not mingling different kinds of seed when they sowed their fields, and not mixing linen and wool in the same garment. But God was providing them metaphors in their daily lives to remind them that He had separated them from the other nations, they were to be different from them. In Leviticus 20:23, He spells it out, "You shall not walk in the manners of the nations which I cast out before you...." and in verse 26, "And you shall be holy unto me, for I the Lord am holy, and I have separated you from other people, that you should be mine."

But despite Israel's vow to God, despite the reminders in their daily lives to be different from the other peoples around them, despite numerous examples of the cost of unfaithfulness, Israel had a long track record of waywardness. They repeatedly worshipped other gods, loved other things before God, and committed spiritual adultery again and again.

But what does this spiritual adultery really look like in action? What did Israel actually *do* to commit idolatry? God describes it in Hosea 2:5, still using Gomer as a metaphor for Israel, "*For their mother has played the whore; she who conceived them has acted shamefully. For she said, 'I will go after my lovers who give me my bread and my water, my wool and my flax, my oil and my drink.*"

All of the nations around Israel worshipped gods other than the One True God. They had physical images made of wood, stone, or metal that they worshipped and made sacrifices to so that the god would send them rain to grow their crops, make their animals thrive, or to give them children. Israel's needs were generously met by God, but for some reason they adopted the gods of the lands around them. They thought those gods would give them what they needed. This was a pattern they repeated over and over. In this particular instance, it was the god called Baal and Asheroth the goddess.

Baal and Asheroth were the god and goddess of fertility, rain, and land. In an agrarian culture, you need the land to be fertile. You need rain for the crops and the animals so that you have oil, bread, and wool. You need these things. And God had provided them bountifully to Israel, but Israel turned her heart and worship to Baal and to Asheroth for the fertility of the land and to give them what they needed, to be their provider of bread and water and oil and the things of life.

So practically speaking, what it means to commit spiritual adultery or idolatry is to look to other things in the world to provide what you need rather than to God. That is the first aspect of idolatry. But there is a second aspect to Israel's idolatry. God says in Hosea 2:8, *"But she did not know that it was I who gave her the grain, the wine, and the oil, and who lavished on her silver and gold, which they used for Baal."* Idolatry is not only looking to other things to give you what only God can give you, but it is giving thanks to other things for what God has given you.

God had made their land fertile. He had blessed them so that they had plenty of bread, wine, and clothing. They had rain and sun in due measure, they had gold and silver in plenty. They were well provided for by a loving God. And they took the gold and silver God had given them, formed it into images of Baal, and then thanked those idols for their good life! And their spiritual adultery did not end there. In an unbelievable act of repudiation of the great I Am, they actually quit calling God Yahweh.

They called God...*Baal.*

Hosea 2:16 says, "In that day, declares the Lord, you will call me 'My Husband,' and *no longer* will you call me 'My Baal.' [Emphasis mine.] Let me put this in perspective. You are married to a wife who looks to other lovers. Not only does she look to other lovers, but she gives her other lovers thanks for paying the mortgage you paid. And not only does she give thanks to her other lovers for the mortgage that you paid, she calls you by their names.

That is exactly how Israel's idolatry is described in Hosea chapter two. Here is the summary. Israel's idolatry is that Israel cheats on God, credits the false gods for all that she's received, and calls God the name of the other gods.

What a whore! And you and I do the exact same thing – same sin, different day. Ed Welch says it this way, "So it is with modern idolatry, as well. We don't want to be *ruled* by alcohol, drugs, sex, gambling, food, or anything. No, we want these substances or activities to give us what we want: good feelings, a better self-image, a sense of power, or whatever our heart is craving."

We are like Israel. We frequently look to other things to provide for us what only God can. Have you ever thought anything like this: If only my employer would provide for me, if only my spouse would perform for me, if only my government would protect me, if only my teacher would approve of me? Oh, we don't call money, or sex, or satisfaction, or validation "Baal," but nevertheless, we have an idol just like Israel did. In fact, if you want to discover the idols of our day, just look at the stations on television – sports channels, food channels, sex channels, finance channels, politics channels. We have 24-hour channels dedicated to our lovers. We look to politics and money and food to give us the things we desire the most when we have said "I do" to God. That is the same, exact spiritual adultery of the nation of Israel here in Hosea 2.

And what do you think happens when the land is not fertile? Answer: We blame God. We thank the false gods for success, and we blame the real God for suffering. In prosperity we forget God, in adversity we blame God. And in both we forsake God to worship other gods. That is what it's like to be married to you and me. Every one of us is a wayward wife who has loved other things, looked to other things to provide for us, celebrated those things instead of God, and made those things our god.

You may know already what your god is. Or you may not see what you are putting in God's place. Some questions that may help you identify your idol are: What is the thing I am most thankful for? What is the thing that I cannot do without? What is the thing that I am most afraid of losing? Those questions will get you down the path of discovering your other spiritual lover, of discovering the idol of your heart.

Given all of this, how would *you* respond if you were God?

Five

God responds to his unfaithful people in three ways, and each one starts with "therefore," which is an if/then kind of word. When "therefore" shows up in a text, you need to see what went before. So we'll restate it in the language of Hosea. Israel played the whore, *"Therefore I will hedge up her way with thorns, and I will build a wall against her so that she cannot find her paths. She shall pursue her lovers but not overtake them, and she shall seek them but shall not find them. Then she shall say, 'I will go and return to my first husband, for it was better for me then than now."* (Hosea 2:6,7) In other words, God *Removes*.

Israel was worshiping Baal because Israel wanted fertile land. "I want crops and wool and bread and oil and something to drink." She was worshiping Baal because he was called the god of rain and fertility, the source of what she wanted. So, what did God do? He cut off the fertile land: Drought. There were no crops because Israel had forgotten that those things come from God.

Let me translate that into the present day. Because His wife is addicted to pills, he flushes her drugs down the toilet. Because His wife is addicted to driving away, He disables the motor. Because his wife is in love with the economy. He shuts down the economy. So God's first response was to remove the fertility that Israel thought was coming from Baal.

God cut off the flow of blessing to the land of the Northern Kingdom. But God didn't stop there. Israel played the whore, *"Therefore, I will take back my grain in its time and my wine in its season. And I will take away my wool and my flax, which were to cover her nakedness. Now I will uncover her lewdness in the sight of her lovers, and no one shall rescue her out of my hand. And I will put an end to all her mirth, her feasts, her new moons, her Sabbaths, and all her appointed feasts. And I will lay waste her vines and her fig trees of which she said, 'These are my wages which my lovers have given me.' I will make them a forest, and the beasts of the field shall devour them."* God *Reveals.*

God's first response to his wayward wife was to remove the things she was crediting her idol for giving her. But this was not merely punishment, it was a correction, a lesson. God is not petty; He doesn't play tit for tat. Israel was believing a lie. She was looking to Baal to meet her needs for food, wool, wine, and flax. God revealed to her that her lover, Baal, didn't have the juice. He was a bad lover. When God removed the fertile land, it revealed that Baal was a terrible provider. God didn't just tell Israel the truth, He *showed* her the truth that Baal *could not* meet her needs.

The whole point of her idolatry was looking to other lovers to get what she wanted, namely, a fertile land. So when God removed the fertility that *He* had provided, that revealed that those lovers had made promises that they could not fulfill. She began to see that "The wine you're drinking," as Dave Matthews says, "ends up drinking you." It doesn't fulfill what it promises. And she realized that Baal couldn't give her what she wanted Baal to give her. To put that another way, she realized that what she wanted was not sourced from Baal. Today, if you look to the economy to provide for your needs and the economy tanks, you realize pretty quickly that the economy is a bad lover.

God's second response reveals to his wayward wife, and to us, the unsatisfactory nature of false gods. I am pretty sure that neither of God's first two responses have been particularly surprising. His third one, though, just blows my mind. First He *removes* so that He can *reveal*, which is to give Him the opportunity to do the unbelievable. This time the "therefore" doesn't refer back to Israel playing the whore. This time it refers back to God's first two responses. God removed her blessings and revealed her false lovers' impotence. Then God shows her His intentions, "*Therefore, behold, I will allure her, and bring her into the wilderness, and speak tenderly to her.*" (Hosea 2:14) God *Romanced* her!

What the removing and the revealing was all intended to do was to get His whoring wife, this unfaithful wife, to the point where God could romance her, where He could wine and dine her. God seduces His wife. He speaks tenderly to her; He takes her out for a candlelight dinner; He doesn't even expect her to sleep on the couch! Do you see the power of this metaphor? Israel not only ran after a new lover, she had multiple lovers. She not only had multiple lovers, she looked to them as her main provider. And not only that, she thanked them instead of God. Then, she even called the one true and living

God the name of the false god. And how did the faithful husband respond to His unfaithful, ungrateful, whoring wife?

He took her out and celebrated their anniversary. Hosea 2:15. *"And there I will give her her vineyards and make the Valley of Achor* [a valley of affliction] *a door of hope. And there she shall answer as in the days of her youth, as at the time when she came out of the land of Egypt,"* the anniversary of when God married his people. He continues.

> *"And in that day, declares the Lord, you shall call me 'My Husband' and no longer call me 'My Baal.' I will remove the names of the Baals from her mouth and they shall be remembered by name no more. And I will make for them a covenant on that day with the beasts of the field, and the birds of the heavens, and the creeping things of the ground. And I will abolish the bow, the sword, and war from the land, and I will make you lie down in safety. And I will betroth you to me forever. I will betroth you to me in righteousness and in justice, in steadfast love and in mercy. I will betroth you to me in faithfulness. And you shall know the Lord.*

That, is the outrageous love of God. His response is to tenderly woo them back to Him so that He can pour out His boundless love on them. It's outrageous. No – actually it's not. It's magnificent. It's sublime. It is transcendent. It is a whole thesaurus of resplendent. And as you come to realize just how extravagant the love of God really is, even for those who have betrayed and rejected Him so utterly and intimately, realize also that this is the same love He has for you.

Gomer and Hosea, the Metaphor Continues

The book of Hosea began with the Lord instructing Hosea to take a prostitute to wife and to have children with her because Hosea and Gomer would be a living metaphor to bring God's message to Israel about Israel's spiritual adultery. Then God revealed what He would do to Israel because of their unfaithfulness, which was idolatry, and what His end goal was as the faithful husband in regard to His unfaithful wife.

In Hosea chapter three, we return to Hosea and Gomer. "And the Lord said to me, '*Go, show your love to your wife again, though she is loved by another man and is an adulteress. Love her as the Lord loves the Israelites, though they turn to other gods and love the sacred raisin cakes.' So I bought her for 15 shekels of silver and about a homer and a lethech of barley.* [About nine bushels] *Then I told her, 'You are to live with me many days; you must not be a prostitute or be intimate with another man, and I will behave the same way toward you.*" (Hosea 3:1-3 NIV).

Here we find Hosea, the faithful husband, apparently a single father, and Gomer, the unfaithful wife, who has left her husband. Not only that, she has also gone back to prostitution. The imagery in chapter three is that Gomer has now returned to the auction block. You can imagine the crowd of men that has gathered around, each one ready to take their turn.

The bidding starts as a man calls, "I'll bid four shekels of silver." Another man yells, "I'll bid five." Another man shouts, "I'll give six." And then, all of a sudden, from the back of the crowd booms the voice of a loving husband, "15 shekels and a homer and lethech of barley." The sudden silence is loud. "Sold." The single word drops into the quiet.

Everyone in the crowd is stunned. Who would pay that for a prostitute? And Gomer starts the shameful walk back to Hosea, clothes ripped, blood on her body. She is limping because of all of her activity. Hosea comes forward to wrap her in his arms, his heart overflowing with eagerness to take her *home* to love her like she has never been loved before. *That* is the love of God for His people.

Do you realize what that is symbolizing? God paying for a prostitute. That is exactly what Hosea does. He buys Gomer, this prostitute of a wife, back into his possession so he can love her fully. That is the boundless love of God for you in the person of Jesus Christ. Do you feel that? I mean, do you really feel that? Because that is the truth. That is the real truth behind the lyrics of that old hymn, Victory in Jesus, when you sing that "He sought me and bought me with His redeeming blood." We sing those lyrics so flippantly.

Do you know what is behind that line, He sought you and bought you with His redeeming blood? It is God, through the cross, purchasing a prostitute. That is what is behind those lyrics, through this imagery of Hosea. The price of our prostitution was crucifixion. The price of our idolatry and sin was the purchase of God's people through the death of his Son.

This literally happened. There really was a man named Hosea and a whoring wife whom he went and bought back. But it is also painting a picture for us that is preparing us for Jesus Christ. Because the truth is, we are Gomer. We have forsaken our marriage to God. We have turned to other lovers. And yet when we were placed on the auction block of salvation and one lover said, "I'll pay four," and another lover said, "I'll pay six," the voice of a loving, faithful husband shouted from the background, "I'll pay it all," with three nails and a cross. And through the crucifixion of Jesus Christ, God purchased us for His love.

That is the good news of the gospel of Jesus Christ. And that truth is more than a metaphor.

Six

When I was growing up, there was an actor/comedian who was at the top of his game on television and in the movies. He was famous for his role on *Saturday Night Live*, and classics like *Groundhog Day* and *Caddyshack*. I'm referring, of course, to Bill Murray. Bill was one of my favorite comedians and one of his movies that I enjoyed most of all was a movie called *What About Bob?* In this dark comedy Bill Murray played a disturbed character who suffered from a cornucopia of phobias. According to Bob, he had obsessive compulsive disorder, a panic disorder, he was a hypochondriac, and he suffered from separation anxiety.

Thankfully for Bob, he met a man by the name of Dr. Leo Marvin. He was a published psychiatrist, and Bob became convinced that Dr. Marvin could fix him; Dr. Marvin would solve all of his issues. But then a problem occurred. Dr. Marvin informed Bob that he and his family were going to go away for several weeks on vacation. Bob would have to see one of Dr. Marvin's colleagues. In addition to that, Dr. Marvin gave Bob *very specific instruction* that Bob was *not* to contact him, in any way whatsoever, at any point while he was on vacation.

But Bob couldn't help himself. Bob couldn't follow the rules. He called Dr. Marvin several times, once actually pretending to be the Doctor's sister. Then he even went so far as to show up in person....

Bob:	*Don't be mad.*
Doctor:	*Bob, your behavior is completely inappropriate.*
Bob:	*You're angry.*
Doctor:	*No, no, I don't get angry.*
Bob:	*Well, you're upset.*
Doctor:	*I don't get upset.*
Bob:	*Well then, let's have a little talk.*
Doctor:	*Bob. I do not see patients on vacation. Ever. How many ways can I make that clear? Now, what I'd like you to do is to get on this bus and go back to New York.*
Bob:	*I can't. I'm totally paralyzed. I'm all locked up.*
Doctor:	*You got yourself here.*
Bob:	*Barely.*
Doctor:	*Well, getting back will be therapeutic.*
Bob:	*But can't we just have a little talk?*
Doctor:	*Bob, you are testing my patience.*

Bob: Come on. I've come so far. I'm baby-stepping. I'm doing the work. I'm baby-stepping. I'm not a slacker.

Doctor: Listen to me.

Bob: Check it out. Look at it. I'm in really bad shape. Come on, please! Please, gimme, gimme, gimme, I need, I need, I need, I need. Gimme, gimme, please!

Doctor: Alright, alright, alright! It's two o'clock. Go to the bus station, buy yourself a ticket home and then wait for me.

Can you relate to Bob? I don't mean do you have a phobia or anxiety issues necessarily. I mean, have you ever reverted to old patterns or behaviors and did what you knew you shouldn't do, what you had been specifically told *not* to do? For instance, maybe you promised your spouse you would stop drinking, but you took a drink anyway. Or your doctor gave you a diet plan that you were to follow religiously, but you just couldn't resist the junk food. You knew you couldn't afford a purchase, but you purchased it anyway? Or you knew that you needed to slow down from your busy lifestyle, but it just never happened. Look, we *all* know exactly what it's like to know what to do and yet fail to do it.

That is also true when it comes to the issue of sin. We know what God has commanded us to do. We know what God has instructed us to do and not do. He has made it very clear. And yet, we go ahead and do the opposite. We are not alone in that, either. The Apostle Paul, for instance, says this in Romans 7:15, 18b, *"For I do not understand my own actions. For I do not do what I want, but I do the very thing I hate….For I have the desire to do what is right, but not the ability to carry it out. For I do not do the good I want, but the evil I do not want is what I keep doing."* Do you understand exactly what that is like, to want to do what is right and yet to fail, repeatedly, to do it?

And it was not only the apostle Paul. The apostle Peter struggled, as well. This is what Paul said of Peter in Galatians 2:11, *"But when Cephas* [Peter] *came to Antioch, I opposed him to his face because he stood condemned. For before certain men came from James, he was eating with the Gentiles; but when they came he drew back and separated himself, fearing the circumcision party. And the rest of the Jews acted hypocritically along with him, so that even Barnabas was led astray by their hypocrisy. But when I saw that their conduct was not in step with the truth of the gospel, I said to Cephas before them all, 'If you, though a Jew, live like a Gentile and not like a Jew, how can you force the Gentiles to live like Jews?'"*

That was Peter, "the Rock," the apostle Peter, who was called out as a hypocrite by the apostle Paul, because he knew what to do and yet failed to do it. *All* of us are just like Bob. We have been given clear instructions, but we slip back into cycles and patterns of disobedience that go against God's commands. And that is exactly what the nation of Israel did here in the book of Hosea. Israel, like Bob, like Paul, like Peter, and like we do, turned their back on the instructions and commands of God.

Hosea 4:1-2 says, *"Hear the word of the Lord, O children of Israel, for the Lord has a controversy with the inhabitants of the land. There is no faithfulness or steadfast love, and no acknowledgment of God in the land. There is swearing, lying, murder, stealing, and committing adultery; they break all bounds, and bloodshed follows bloodshed.*

Unfaithful

This was a summary of the waywardness that was taking place within the nation of Israel. God gave three specific issues, or points of controversy, that He had with His people. Issue one: They disobeyed the law. Israel was a bride who said, "I do," but didn't. She continued to disobey and be unfaithful to the law of God. The sins mentioned in verse two are all violations of the Ten Commandments, which were what the nation of Israel said "I do" to: "Yes. *All that the Lord has spoken we will do.*" That was the first controversy, or issue, that God had with the people of Israel.

Unloving

Issue two: Their love was not steadfast. Israel had no love for God. She was a wife that had no feeling, no affection, no passion for her husband. The thrill was gone. This is further explained in Hosea 6:4, "*What shall I do with you, O Ephraim?*" [Northern Kingdom] "*What shall I do with you, O Judah?* [Southern Kingdom] "*Your love is like a morning cloud, like the dew that goes early away.*"

The metaphor, the imagery there is that their love was like fog in the morning, there for a short time, but quickly faded away. Now look at what God said in verse six. "*For I desire steadfast love and not sacrifice, the knowledge of God rather than burnt offerings.*" In other words, Israel, you're just going through the motions. You're offering up sacrifices, you're making burnt offerings, but your heart isn't in it. The sacrifices and offerings are meaningless without your love. I want more than routine action; I want real affection. I want your love.

Israel was in a loveless marriage to her God. She was going through the motions, but there was no real affection for God. Her love was like the morning fog that was there for a moment and then quickly vanished away. Have you ever been there spiritually, just going through the motions with no real affection for God? Jonathan Edwards, the 18th-century pastor and theologian, described that state in this way, "He who has no religious affection is in a state of spiritual death and is wholly destitute of the powerful, quickening, saving influences of the Spirit of God upon his heart." That was the state of the Kingdom of Israel, a bride who had violated her vows: spiritually dead and with no affection for her God.

Unyielding

Issue three: They refused God's lordship; they wouldn't acknowledge the One True God. They knew who God was. Their Torah was all about Yahweh. The issue was not that they didn't understand who He was; the issue was that they wouldn't accede to His lordship. They simply acted like they didn't know God existed. It was a repudiation of the authority of God Almighty. Of course they knew who God was, their posture here was an I-don't-care-what-you-say, attitude. Have your children ever done that? "I don't care what you say, I'm going to do what I want to do." That was exactly what Israel was doing. They were refusing to acknowledge that the Creator has a right – every right – to tell His creatures what to do and what not to do. They wouldn't acknowledge the extreme grace of the Creator for singling them out from all of the peoples of the Earth as His own precious possession. No, they essentially said, "Talk to the hand," unmindful that He had created their hands and everything else, and then they went off and bowed down to false gods and ran down the road to destruction.

So, here's the SITREP, the situation report, of Israel's relationship with God: Israel had broken her vows to obey God fully and keep His covenant (Exodus 19:5). She had no affection for God, though she was going through the motions. And she wouldn't acknowledge God's authority in her life.

No wonder God had issues with His people.

The question now becomes, why was Israel behaving so badly? Look at Hosea 5:3, *"I know Ephraim, and Israel is not hidden from me. For now, Ephraim* [Northern Kingdom]*, you have played the whore; Israel is defiled. Their deeds do not permit them to return to their God for the spirit of whoredom is within them, and they know not the Lord."* They've gone so far now, they don't even know the way back. They just can't help themselves now.

This was the source of their waywardness, namely, that they were worshiping other gods. We have talked about the imagery of whoredom, and how it is a metaphor for idolatry, seeking other gods above Yahweh: Baal, Asheroth, security, money, etc. But that is not where their waywardness *began.*

Seven

Before sin is an action of the hands, it is an affection of the heart. This is *critically* important. Before sin is ever an action of the hands, that is, something that you *do*, it is an affection of the heart. For example, if you long for recognition, you may lie and twist the truth to make yourself look better. The desire of your heart led to the bad behavior. If you want to be loved, you may do unhealthy things to your body to be attractive. If you crave security, you may obsess about money and refuse to be generous. In the same way, Israel was behaving badly because inwardly, she loved other things more than she loved God.

It is interesting that in church life, and in Christian life, and in counseling, we almost always focus on the action rather than the affection. You see, your issue is not pornography. Your issue is not anger. Your issue is not lying. Your issue is not being constantly obsessed with the size of your backside. Those are not your issues. Your issue is that within you there is a longing, an affection for something to be your god, to play the role of God in your life. And that is why you act out in those ways. Behaviors are nothing more than the warning lights on the dashboard of your life pointing you to what your functional god is, the desire that you have made your god. If you really want to correct the behavior or the action, you've got to follow the *affection*. Jesus said, and I'm paraphrasing, if you want to know where your heart is, look for what you treasure. [Matthew 6:21]

So do a deep dive into your soul. What do you love? What do you *really* love? What are your goals? What really matters to you? What makes you feel safe? What makes you feel successful? What do you dream about? What do you talk the most about? What do you spend most of your time and money on? What is it that your heart really, truly loves?

This is what JRR Tolkien was trying to describe and illustrate in the Lord of the Rings with the ring itself. This ring that becomes your obsession. This ring that will give you what you want. If I could just get the ring, I'd have power, it would answer all my questions, it would solve all my problems.

For Israel, their ring, the thing they *had* to have, their obsession, their heart's affection – was prosperity. "Look at how well things are going. Look at how prosperous the land is." And that is what led them to the behavior of worshiping Baal. So, Israel was unfaithful, she had no affection for Yahweh, and she didn't recognize His authority, so she had other gods on the side. Why? Because the other gods promised her prosperity.

The God Whose Love Hurts and Heals

How did God respond? How did God respond to a wife who was behaving badly, who not only had hands that were sinning, but a heart that was wayward and sinful? Hosea 5:9, "*Ephraim shall become a desolation in the day of punishment; among the tribes of Israel I make known what is sure. The princes of Judah have become like those who move the landmark. Upon them I will pour out my wrath like water. Ephraim is oppressed, crushed in judgment because he was determined to go after filth.*"

Suffering was coming Israel's way. And Israel cannot claim that she wasn't warned. You remember God telling Hosea back in chapter one, to name the first child of his unfaithful wife Jezreel, which meant "bloodshed" because of the bloody history of the Valley of Jezreel. And to name the next two children, No Mercy and Not My People. God warned of coming judgment for several years, perhaps a decade. The book of Hosea repeatedly talks about how the discipline of God was going to come from Assyria. And we know historically that Assyria did, indeed, descend on the Northern Kingdom in 722 BC, and there was great bloodshed, and they carried off most of the people. In other words, God wounded his wayward wife. This was the discipline of God.

Sometimes hardship and suffering are the cause-and-effect results of disobedience, as it was so often for Israel, but that is not always so. Recently I was talking with a friend over breakfast, and he was sharing how he lost his wife to a long medical battle several years earlier. He told me that it wasn't because of any sin that he or she or his family had done that she died. And as he was suffering through his grief, he remembered a time when he looked to

God and he said, "God, you hurt me. You cut me. You wounded me through this suffering." But, he told me, he really learned through that process of God wounding him and cutting him, bringing suffering into his life, that the seemingly senseless disaster was the love of God, that God was doing a work in his life. He learned things about who God was that he never would have learned any other way. You see, like a surgeon, God cuts his people to bring about good in their life.

That is what He was doing here with the nation of Israel. The cutting was a judgment because of their sin, but it was still a cutting to bring about healing. God said it was coming and it did. And how did Israel respond to this warning of judgment and discipline from God? They went crazy. Hosea 5:13, *"When Ephraim saw his sickness and Judah his wound, then Ephraim went to Assyria and sent to the Great King. But he is not able to cure you or heal your wound."*

Israel realized they were in trouble, realized that they were in a mess. And instead of going to God for healing, she ran to other gods again. She went to the king of Assyria. [Side note: In the ancient near east, Kings were often seen as either gods or a vessel of the gods.] And so, in a very real way, Israel ran to other gods saying, Can you get me out of this mess? Can you get me out of this wounding? Assyria had gained ascendency as a nation in that area of the world. They were swallowing other smaller nations around them. So, politically, Israel reached out to see if they could make some kind of an agreement where Assyria would not bother them.

God was going to discipline Israel by wounding them, but instead of repenting and asking God for healing, Israel ran to something else to bring healing in her life. And we do the same thing, do we not? God cuts us and we run to alcohol. God cuts us and we run to money. God cuts us and we run to family thinking maybe they can heal us, maybe they can make things better. Most of us run to false doctors rather than to the Great Physician. But what you learn, and what Israel learned in verse 13, is this, "*He* [the Assyrian king] *is not able to cure you.*" None of the gods are able to help you. Only God can do that. This reminds me of a story about Gerald Barnes.

Gerald Barnes was a chief physician at a very prominent health clinic. He was loved by his patients. He was admired by many of his colleagues. But there was a big problem with Gerald: He wasn't a doctor. He was a con artist. You see, in the late 1970s, Gerald changed his name to impersonate an orthopedic surgeon in California. Later when he was discovered, court documents revealed that he had performed medical examinations on hundreds of other patients. Things started to unravel when a 29-year-old man came to him complaining of diabetic symptoms and was prescribed drugs for vertigo. Two days later, that patient was found dead because of a diabetic coma. False doctors provide faulty solutions. Assyria can't save you. Money can't save you, family can't heal you. Only the Great Physician can heal you.

Israel committed all these evil things because she was wayward in her heart. So God cut His people like a surgeon to expose the hideous cancer in her core because He loved His people. But instead of turning to Him for their healing, they ran after false doctors. And what they discovered in the process was that the fakers could not heal the wound.

That's exactly what Israel finally realizes. Look at how chapter six begins, "*Come let us return to the Lord for he has torn us* [That is, He's cut us, He's wounded us] *that He may heal us. He has struck us down and he will bind us up.*"

There are wonderful truths in that verse. Two of them are that Israel finally came to her senses and returned at last to the one true and living God. And, even more marvelous, is the truth that God was right there, waiting for them.

He hadn't gone anywhere. He'd been waiting for them to return. Child of God, he hasn't left you. He hasn't given up on you. He hasn't shut the door on you. He hasn't closed his heart to you. No. He is the loving father who is waiting patiently for the prodigal. He is the loving spouse waiting to receive his wayward bride. And when you return, He will love you and heal you of all your wounds.

How do I know? Look at Hosea 6:2, *"After two days he will revive us; and on the third day he will raise us up, that we may live before him."* Does that sound familiar to you? On the third day He will raise us up. How does healing come for Israel and for you? Healing comes through a single Israelite who, unlike Israel and we Christians, was actually faithful to God in every way because He fulfilled the law. This one Israelite who, unlike Israel and we, actually loved His father with all His heart. This one single Israelite who, unlike Israel and we, recognized His father's authority, such as when He cried out in the garden of Gethsemane. "Not my will, but Your will be done."

Jesus is the true and greater Israel. Jesus was everything Israel was not, and is everything we are not. And on the cross, Jesus was wounded for their unfaithfulness and our unfaithfulness so that His faithfulness would be credited to us. As the Bible says, "He was pierced for our transgressions, he was crushed for our iniquities. The punishment that brought us peace was upon him, and by his wounds we are healed." [Isaiah 53:5]

Listen, when it comes to the love of God, what about Bob? That is, what about those people who keep doing the very thing they have been told not to do? Answer: They are invited to come to God because God never goes on vacation. He is the faithful spouse and the gracious father who cannot wait to welcome you home.

Eight

She is Not as Pretty as She Looks

I have often heard it said that *No publicity is bad publicity*, but when Brian Kolb made headlines in December of 2019, I think he would have argued with that marketing truism. Kolb was the top Republican in the New York State Assembly where he served for more than 20 years. He made headlines neither for policy he proposed, nor for advocating a call to action. Rather he made headlines because he had been arrested for driving under the influence of alcohol. It was late on New Year's Eve when Kolb and his wife left the Erie Grill in Pittsford to go home, and they were almost there when he crashed his 2018 GMC Acadia into a ditch while making a turn. The Ontario County Sheriff's Department performed a sobriety test on him when they arrived and found his blood alcohol level to be twice the legal limit.

"This was a terrible lapse in judgment," he said, "and one I take full responsibility for." The populace is often tolerant when a politician owns up to a bad mistake, but not this time. Kolb faced a harsh public backlash, not so much for driving drunk, though it was irresponsible, but for driving drunk after he had made this public statement literally days before. "Many of our holiday traditions, especially our New Year's Eve celebrations, involve indulging in spirits. Done safely and in moderation, these can be wonderful experiences. However, tragedy can be only one bad decision away." What caused such outrage among the hard-drinking New Yorkers was not just his personal irresponsibility, it was his public hypocrisy.

Do you know a hypocrite? Surely you've experienced someone that you would consider a hypocrite. It might be the realtor who told you, "I despise those realtors who don't weed out houses that don't meet the buyer's wish list," when he, himself, pays no attention to anything but the bed/bath numbers. Or maybe you have that kid who tells her Instagram followers, "Oh, I just hate fakes," but you know she colors her hair and uses filters on her camera. Or the college student who says, "Yeah, I'm committed to making all A's," when in reality he's spending his time partying. Or maybe even worse, a Christian who acts like they have it all together when their private life is a mess.

Hypocrisy bothers us to our core, doesn't it? Like the old band, the Beastie Boys, used to sing as I was growing up in high school, "Your dad caught you smoking and he says, no way, but that hypocrite smokes two packs a day." Hypocrisy. It's something that bothers us and it is exactly what bothers God in Hosea 6. That is the issue that God is addressing with the people of Israel.

Look at Hosea 6:4, '*What shall I do with you, Ephraim? What shall I do with you, Judah?*"

Have you ever looked at your spouse or child or friend and shaken your head, saying, "What am I going to do with you?" You've said that, haven't you? I'm sure you've had that reaction, which means, "I've tried everything I know to do, but you won't respond. You won't do what's right. What am I going to do with you?" I'm sure God feels that way many times with us.

That is how God felt about Israel at this point in the book of Hosea. "I have threatened discipline, Israel, and I have promised restoration, but you're still not responding. You're still doubling down on your idols." And be honest, wouldn't you have given up on them by now? You've even given up on yourself, occasionally, haven't you? Fortunately, God's love is not like our love. His love, as we've seen throughout this book, is boundless, there's no quit in it.

Here is the wonderful truth, what is so incredible about God's love is that once you belong to Him, once you are in relationship with him, He will never cut you off. He will never let you go. And the reason that is the case is because God knew who you were when He chose to love you. God knew everything about who you are and who you would be when He said, "I do." Your waywardness has never, *ever*, not even for a second, caught Him by surprise. Let me prove this to you.

Look back at Hosea 3:1, "*And the Lord told me,* [Hosea] *go show your love to your wife again, though she is loved by another man and is an adulteress. Love her as the Lord loves the Israelites, though they turn to other gods and love the sacred raisin cakes.*" Hosea is told to go love a woman and he already knows the type of woman she is when he marries her. It's not like he gets into the relationship and buys her back and then is like, "Oh. I didn't know you were prostituting yourself." No, Hosea knows that about Gomer from the get-go. And, of course, Hosea and Gomer illustrate the relationship between God and His people, meaning He already knew the kind of wife you would be when He married you.

That is why His love will never cut you off. That is why His love will never go away. He knew exactly everything there is to know about you the moment you entered into relationship with Him. He does not get ten years down the road with you and say, "Well, I sure didn't see that coming." His love is outrageous because from before the beginning, He knew exactly the kind of bride you would be. So here in chapter six, we discover a different aspect of Israel's sin, of Israel's unfaithfulness: Her hypocrisy. Hosea 6:6, "*For I desire steadfast love, not sacrifice, and acknowledgment of God,* [recognition of God's authority] *rather than burnt offerings.*"

I mentioned in the last chapter that one of the things that Israel is continuing to do is to go through the external motions, she is continuing to offer sacrifices and burnt offerings to God. So she's putting on the *form* of sanctity and obedience while in her *heart* she is worshiping other gods. Let me return to the metaphor that runs throughout the book of Hosea to show exactly the hypocrisy that is being addressed here.

1. Israel married God at Mount Sinai, saying "We do." [Exodus 19]
2. Israel broke her vows. [Hosea 4:2] She broke *all* of the commandments that she promised to uphold.
3. Israel had other lovers, she went after other gods.

4. Israel had no affection for God, for her husband, there was no love. [Hosea 4:1, and 6:6] It was a loveless marriage.

5. Israel did not acknowledge God's care or authority. [Hosea 4:1, 6:6]

6. Israel called God by the name of Baal. [Hosea 2:16]

7. Israel ran to Baal, not God, in times of suffering. [Hosea 5:13]

8. Israel pretended she was still the perfect spouse. She acted like nothing had changed, that she was still faithful to Yahweh.

Here you have all of the clear examples of Israel's unfaithfulness to God, and yet, by continuing to offer sacrifices and burnt offerings, she was trying to convince God that she was still faithful. Hypocrite, hypocrite, hypocrite.

This shows us what hypocrisy is and what hypocrisy is *not*. I think folks often misunderstand what hypocrisy is. For instance, it is not hypocritical if you still go to church on Sunday when you've sinned during the week. Everybody who goes to church has sinned during the week, that's not hypocrisy, that is the human condition. Hypocrisy is *pretending* that you're better than that. Saying you haven't sinned when you have is a lie. Hypocrisy goes a step further and puts on the *appearance* of virtue without repenting of the sin and turning away from it. Hypocrisy is not that there *is* a gap between what you say and what you do. Hypocrisy is *hiding* the gap.

Nine

Nothing to See Here, Move Along

Hypocrisy is when you try to convince God, yourself, and/or others that there really *is no gap*, that you are actually not as bad as you know you are. Hypocrisy is when you see that you are a mess, you see your sin, but instead of acknowledging your sin and resting in the boundless love of God, you try to cover up that mess with moral activity. You try to cover up that mess with giving some money in the offering, or with your church attendance, or increasing your community service. You do those outward sacrifices, those outward actions as a way to try to convince yourself, and convince those around you, and maybe even convince God that you're not that big of a mess after all.

And that is why Jesus would rather have lunch with a prostitute than he would a Pharisee. Why? Because she is willing to admit she's sick. She is willing to admit she's a mess. Let me give you three aspects of religious hypocrisy that we see here in Hosea to help us understand what religious hypocrisy is, why God hates it, and why it is anti-gospel.

"But I'm Doing All the Right Things"

Israel was putting in the work. She was doing the observances that she had been doing since God led her out of Egypt, back when she still had a heart for Yahweh, back when she still loved Him. But in Hosea 6:4, God says, "*What shall I do with you, O Ephraim? What shall I do with you, O Judah? Your love is like a morning cloud, like the dew that goes early away. Therefore, I have hewn them by the prophets; I have slain them by the words of my mouth, and my judgment goes forth as the light. For I desire steadfast love and not sacrifice, the knowledge of God rather than burnt offerings.*" Israel offered sacrifices and burnt offerings to God while seeking security from the world and its gods. Israel was still following the outward observances of God's law, but something had changed.

Look back at Hosea 5:13, "*Now, when Ephraim saw his sickness* [he saw his sin] *and Judah his wound, then Ephraim turned to Assyria and sent to the great king. But he cannot cure you or heal your wound.*" In other words, Israel realized their waywardness. Israel understood their betrayal of God and His law. They saw that they had done everything they had promised that they would not do. They looked in the mirror and saw themselves as they really were, but what did they do? How did they respond? They ran to *Assyria* for security – while continuing to offer sacrifices to God. Israel was performing religious activities

66

with a heart that didn't love God. We can change external behavior without loving God. That's the problem.

"Pay No Attention to the Man Behind the Curtain"

Israel tried to *look* clean even though she was foul. Hosea 6:10, "*In the house of Israel I have seen a horrible thing; Ephraim's whoredom is there; Israel is defiled.*" Again, the metaphor is marriage and the language used throughout the book has to do with the betrayal of marriage: Prostitution, whoredom, defilement. God is saying Israel, His beloved bride, is unclean, she is defiled, she is filthy. So she has two options: She can either come to God for cleansing, or she can just put lipstick on the pig and try to look good. Israel chose the latter. Through her religious activity of offering sacrifices and burnt offerings, she's trying to *look* as though she's true and faithful and virtuous even though her heart is faithless, wayward, and filthy. But God sees what is in the heart.

Imagine that you own a car that has a nice body but the engine is falling apart – it's a total disaster underneath the hood. But rather than taking it to the mechanic to have it restored, what you do instead is clean the outside until it's spotless and shiny in hopes that when other people look at the car, they'll be impressed. And some people might be fooled – but not the mechanic. Ten thousand car washes will not fix your engine.

Israel was trying to buff up her image to hide the defilement in her heart. But the problem was not the dirt on her hands, it was the depravity in her heart. *Our* problem is not the dirt on our hands, it is the depravity of our hearts. It's an internal problem, not external.

It is similar to one of my favorite movies, The Godfather. There is a scene when Michael Corleone is standing as godfather to a child being baptized. The Catholic priest asks him, "Do you renounce Satan and all of his works?" And Michael Corleone says, "Yes, I renounce him," and the ceremony continues. But the film cuts back and forth between Corleone going through this religious activity, and scene after scene where he has given the order to kill all these people. In other words, externally, he's in the right place, he's in church. He's saying all the right words, "Yes, I renounce the works of Satan." But internally, he still has the heart of a murderer.

Let me give you a couple of examples from Jesus's ministry that illustrate this from both sides. The first is found in Matthew 23:25 where Jesus says, "*Woe to you, scribes and Pharisees, hypocrites! For you clean the outside of the cup and the plate, but inside they are full of greed and self-indulgence. You blind Pharisee! First clean the inside of the cup and the plate, that the outside also may be clean. Woe to you, scribes and Pharisees, hypocrites! For you are like whitewashed tombs, which outwardly appear beautiful, but within are full of dead people's bones and all uncleanness. So you also outwardly appear righteous to others, but within you are full of hypocrisy and lawlessness.*" That's what Jesus said about the Pharisees. And it is exactly what Israel was doing a few hundred years earlier as recorded in Hosea. They were trying to look clean through their sacrifices when inwardly they were dreadfully unclean.

Now let's compare that to a different encounter with Jesus. Luke 5:12, "*While he* [Jesus] *was in one of the cities, there came a man full of leprosy.* [So, an unclean man] *And when he saw Jesus, he fell on his face and begged him, 'Lord, if you will, you can make me clean.' And Jesus stretched out his hand and touched him, saying, 'I will; be clean.' And immediately the leprosy left him."* That is a very different response than what we saw in the first example. In the first example, the Pharisees were trying to appear clean when, in reality, they were not, whereas the leper acknowledged he was unclean and that the only one who could make him clean was Jesus.

The reason God hates religious hypocrisy is because it presumes that *you* can clean what only *God* can, that your activity is sufficient to fix what only God can restore. Religion is when you use soap to clean the skin. Repentance is when the Spirit regenerates us within.

Ten

"I'll Scratch Your Back if You Scratch Mine"

In the first century, the Apostle Paul wrote to Timothy about people who have *"a form of godliness but deny the power that could make them godly."* (II Timothy 3:5) That's a great description of Israel during Hosea's time. Israel put on the appearance of contrition, going through the motions of worship to Yahweh, while actually trying to control Him. Back in Hosea 2:14, God told Hosea, *"Therefore, behold, I will allure her and bring her into the wilderness and speak tenderly to her."* And in verse 16 Hosea continued, *"And in that day, declares the Lord, you will call me My Husband and no longer will you call me My Baal."* In other words, Israel was worshiping God, the one true and living God, the same way that she was worshiping Baal. So, how was Baal worship different from the worship of the Most High? After all, every god requires sacrifice, right? The question is, what kind of sacrifice?

Before the Messiah came, Israel sacrificed very specific things in very specific ways, and everything was symbolic of Israel's "calling out" from the rest of the world and being a sanctified people, for the Messiah would enter humanity through them. Their sacrifices were a rolling forward of their sins until the day the Messiah became the ultimate Sacrifice who would pay the price for all. Yahweh did not bargain with His people. They were not made for *His* convenience. His plan was to be here for *them*, for *us*, to redeem us all.

Different gods claimed or were given different attributes like fertility, storms, war, etc. The sacrifices required for the god's favor varied. Baal worship often involved sex with a temple prostitute. The sacrifice could be blood, even human blood; it could be a slave; it could be food; it could be money. There are still some cultures today that offer up acts of sacrifice like these in hopes that their ancestors, or the gods, or whatever, will do what the supplicant wants them to do. "I'm offering this sacrifice in order to make you happy, so you'll give me what I want."

Israel was worshiping God in that way, not as an offering of love, obedience, and gratitude, but as a way to get what they wanted from God. In the 1978 Burt Reynolds movie called *The End,* the main character has bungled a suicide attempt and he's now all alone in this big body of water and wants to be rescued, so he starts a conversation with God. This was his prayer.

"I can never make it. Help me, Lord, please. If I promise not to try and kill myself anymore, save me and I swear I'll be a better father. I'll be a

better man. I'll be a better everything. All I ask is make me a better swimmer. Oh God, I can't do this to Julie. We can't do this to Julie.

Oh God, let me live and I promise to obey every one of the Ten Commandments: I shall not kill, I shall not commit adultery, I shall not – I'll – I'll learn the ten commandments, and then I'll obey every one of 'em. Just get me back to the beach. I'll be honest in business. I promise not to sell lakeside lots unless there's a lake around.

I want to see another sunrise. I want to see another sunset. It was a mistake, God, I never really wanted to kill myself. I just wanted to get your attention. Help me make it. I'll give you 50% of everything I make, 50% God. I want to point out that nobody gives 50%. I'm talking gross, God.

I think I'm going to make it. You won't regret this, Lord, I'll obey every commandment. I'll see my parents more often. No more cheatin' in business – once I get rid of those nine acres in the desert. And I'm going to start donating that 10% right away. I know I said 50%, Lord, but 10% to start. If you don't want your 10%, then don't take it. I know it was you that saved me, but it was also you that made me sick."

And he splashes out onto the beach.

Now, this is meant to be satire, but it makes the point that none of the promises that he made were given out of contrition. It was all about trying to control God. In other words, he didn't really want God, he just wanted to get to dry land. The prayer was an attempt to control or manipulate God into giving him the safety that he wanted. It is very much like one of the criminals who was crucified next to Jesus when he demands, "Save yourself…and US." Meaning, if you were truly the Son of God, you'd do what I ask you to do. That is exactly what Israel was doing. She was not offering the sacrifices because she was genuine in her contrition before God. She was really maneuvering for control to "obligate" God to do what she wanted.

The Hard Truth

We try to manipulate God into doing what we want, too. You don't think so? Ask yourself this. When suffering comes into your life, when something is taken away, do you get mad at God because He owes you something? Do you get mad at God because you don't deserve it? Like the female soccer player who tore her Achilles in her final soccer game. After the game she said, "If there was a god, this proves that there isn't." I mean, look at all the years you've been a Christian. Look at all the things you've done for Him. Look at all the money you've given to kingdom-building programs. Why be a Christian if this is where it gets you? In other words, all that activity was done in an attempt to control God. And the moment you get something you don't want, you're mad at Him.

So, is there hope for hypocrites? Look at Matthew 9:9-11, "*As Jesus passed on from there he saw a man called Matthew sitting at the tax booth, and he said to him, 'Follow me.' And he rose and followed him. And as Jesus reclined at table in the house, behold many tax collectors and sinners came and were reclining with Jesus and his disciples. And when the Pharisees saw this, they said to his disciples, 'Why does your teacher eat with tax collectors and sinners?'"*

Jesus was eating with tax collectors. They were individuals who cheated their own people to kiss up to their Roman overlords. They were traitors. People despised tax collectors. And Jesus was eating with a group of the hated tax collectors and other sinners. The religious leaders were upset. Very upset. How could Jesus do this? Why would He eat with people like that? How can you have a reputable ministry and hang out with such reprobates? Now, watch how Jesus answers their frustration. "But when Jesus heard it, he said, *'Those who are well have no need of a physician, but those who are sick.'"*

Jesus gives the perfectly reasonable answer that it is the sick who are the ones who need a doctor. "My mission," Jesus says, "is for sinners." Then Jesus explains why the Pharisees don't understand it, why they've missed it, why they can't see what Jesus is doing. Jesus then said, "*Go and learn what this means: 'I desire mercy, and not sacrifice.' I came not to call the righteous, but sinners.*" That was a direct quote from Hosea 6:6.

Jesus said to the Pharisees, "The reason you don't understand why I'm eating with tax collectors and prostitutes and sinners is because you haven't learned the lesson of Hosea. You haven't learned the issue that Israel struggled with back in the days of Hosea. In other words, if you had learned that lesson of Hosea 6, you wouldn't question what I'm doing. Namely, the mission of Jesus is not for those who pretend they're not Gomer, but for those who are willing to admit that they are. Christ didn't come for the self-righteous, He came for the sinners. Here is the truth. Jesus would rather marry a whore than a hypocrite. Why? Because the Great Physician came for the sick, not for those who pretend to be healthy. Until we admit we are a mess, we will never be a part of Jesus's kingdom.

Don't be Brian Kolb. Don't be like Israel in Hosea. Don't be like the Pharisees. Don't be a hypocrite, for you will never fully experience the boundless love of God until you stop offering *your* sacrifices and start resting in *His*. After all, Jesus was not humiliated publicly for you to spend your life trying to maintain a public image. Jesus was not broken before God for you to spend your life trying to convince God you've got your life all together. Admit it, you're a whore. And the good news of the gospel is that that is exactly the kind of woman Jesus wants to marry.

Eleven

A Roadmap to Repentance

It was an early March morning when Albert and his wife Rita loaded their Chevy Astro van and headed out from their home in British Columbia, Canada. Their destination on this road trip was Las Vegas, Nevada. Albert was scheduled to attend a trade show there for his job, but rather than go the usual direct route, Albert and Rita decided they'd take the scenic route. They decided they would travel down Highway 51 in Idaho, and then eventually, of course, they'd make their way back to the main road that would take them to Vegas. In fact, a few days before the trip, Albert had purchased a Magellan GPS, but he had never taken it out of the box. And as the trip went on and the day got darker, Albert and Rita realized that they couldn't find the main road. Lost and unable to get back to the main route, they decided that they would consult their GPS.

They assumed that the nearest town was Mountain City, Nevada, and they entered that into the GPS as their destination. The directions then led them down a very small dirt road until, eventually, they came to what was a very confusing three-way split, a crossroads. Based on their GPS, they chose what they thought was the best way to go. Unfortunately, things only got worse. In fact, had Albert been driving during the daytime, he might have noticed that, as he kept driving, he was actually going deeper and deeper into the Jarbidge Mountains. The road kept twisting and turning. It would go down and then back up, and eventually the road got so narrow they couldn't drive any farther. They decided to just stop there for the night. It was too dark to go back.

Albert and Rita never made it to the trade show. In fact, just a few weeks later, the police would call off the search for them that covered four states and over 3000 miles. Two months later, three hunters were passing through that area and they noticed a Chevy Astro van. A woman, near death, struggled to open the sliding van door and stick her head out. It was Rita. She was then airlifted to the hospital where she barely survived. Albert's remains were found several miles away on the side of a mountain as he had journeyed off to find help.

Have you ever been lost? Have you ever veered off course? Have you ever gone astray? I mean, you set out to follow the recipe exactly as it was written, but it didn't quite turn out right. You set out to follow the coach's play exactly as he had instructed, but things fell apart. You tried to follow the instructions that you were given, but things just didn't turn out the way you thought they would. Has that ever happened to you spiritually? Have you ever gotten off course in your spiritual walk with God? You set out to follow the rules, you set out to obey God, you set out to keep your promises, but somewhere along the way in the journey of faith, you found yourself way off course.

That is exactly what happened to the nation of Israel. They had been rescued from Egypt, delivered from Pharaoh's hand. They had been protected through the Red Sea. They had been brought to Mount Sinai where God proposed a covenant with them. He told them, up front, His commands, laid the groundwork of what it would be to live in relationship with Him, and made His offer. And Israel said, we do – and they meant it. They wanted to obey God. They wanted to follow God, they wanted to worship God. But as time went on, Israel drifted, betrayed her marriage vows, and took lovers among the surrounding gods.

And this reality is what is being pictured in the book of Hosea in the literal marriage between Hosea and Gomer. Hosea, the faithful husband, and Gomer, the prostitute wife, a woman who, no doubt, did not set out to be a whore, but drifted over time. And yet in all of that, God never stopped loving His people. Look back to Hosea 2:14 again, "*Therefore, I will allure her and bring her into the wilderness and speak tenderly to her. And there I will give her vineyards and make the Valley of Achor a door of hope. And there she shall answer as in the days of her youth, as at the time when she came out of the land of Egypt.*"

God is wooing back his wayward wife. She has gone astray, she has gone off course, she is out in no man's land worshiping other gods, making idols to those gods. And God wants to bring her back to the right path. He wants to bring her back to Him. And so it is time for Israel to wake up from their waywardness and to realize just how far off course they have become.

What we find in chapters seven, eight, and nine, and even into ten, is God exposing some of the results of their idolatry, helping them to understand what their idolatry really is. This is a very complicated section of scripture. But it is worth the work to get to the effective life application found here. So what I have decided to do is to step back from the text in a very practical way and give you four simple questions to help you to identify the idols in your life, the way that Israel needed to do, so that you can leave your idols in the dust and return to God. That is really what this section is all about. So for each of these questions, I'm going to explain what it meant for Israel, and then we're going to step back and look at how it applies to our lives.

What Are You Emotionally Invested In?

What is your passion? Your passions are a good starting point in identifying your idol(s). I want to remind you that when God says, "They are all adulterers," He is not talking about physical adultery. Using the metaphor of marriage, God is talking about their idolatry.

Hosea 7:7, "*When I restore the fortunes of my people, when I would heal Israel, the iniquity of Ephraim is revealed, and the evil deeds of Samaria, for they deal falsely; the thief breaks in and the bandits raid outside. But they do not consider that I remember all their evil. Now, their deeds surround them; they are before my face. By their evil they make the king glad, and the princes by their treachery. They are all adulterers; they are like a heated oven whose baker ceases to stir the fire, from the kneading of the dough until it is leavened. On the day of our king, the princes became sick with the heat of wine; he stretched out his hand with mockers. For with hearts like an oven they approach their intrigue; all night their anger smolders; in the morning, it blazes like a flaming fire. All of them are hot as an oven, and they devour their rulers. All their kings have fallen and none of them calls upon me."*

What is God describing? We know from verse four that God is describing Israel's idolatry. And then He gives another metaphor to illustrate it, an image of an oven that keeps getting hotter and hotter. The baker has stopped tending the fire while they are doing other things, and it is roaring. Their hearts are like this oven.

In other words, there is a burning passion that has gone out of control. Johnny Cash sang about this kind of passion in Ring of Fire, do you remember the lyrics of that song? "I fell into a burning ring of fire. I go down, down, down, but the flames go higher." That's exactly what Hosea 7:4 is talking about, this burning passion that is out of control and consuming their lives.

Israel's out-of-control passions were consuming the lives of others, as well. In verse three, God speaks of the King and of treacherous princes. In verse seven, He says, "They devour their rulers, their kings have fallen." In this time period, Israel had six kings in about ten years, and four of them were assassinated. In other words, people were burning with this passion for power, political power, and they wanted that power so much that it was literally leading to murder. Kings were dying because of this passion gone out of control. This text is teaching that their passion for political power had become their idol. Their passion was off course with God. It had gotten so out of control, like a fire in an oven, that it was leading them astray.

Don't get me wrong, passions are great. There's nothing wrong with passion. God has given you passions. That's a good thing. The danger occurs when your passion becomes consuming. When you are like the burning oven here in Hosea 7, that is when it has become an idol. That is when it has become a God in your life. Let me give you some examples.

You can be passionate about sports, many people are passionate about sports, and that is no problem in and of itself. The problem is that passion for a sports team, that passion for competition, can become so consuming that it leads you to act out in sinful ways. Your team loses and you're gutted. You throw things. Your family walks in and you're like, "Get out of here! Leave me alone!" You're acting out against others. Or your team loses and you just disappear for days. In other words, your passion, which in and of itself would be okay, has burned out of control so much that it is actually impacting others around you, it is leading you to sin. That is when you know it has become an idol. Think of it this way, your passion for sports has become greater than your passion for God. It has a hold on your life. It is consuming you in some way.

So ask yourself, what am I emotionally invested in? What are those things that I am really passionate about, but passionate in a way that can lead to unhealthiness, sinful things? It could be politics. Have you looked at the culture we're living in right now? I mean, politics is ablaze. People are outraged when it comes to politics because politics is their God. Or your passion could be respect, or environmentalism, or science. It could be your pets, or music, or fashion, or food, or fitness. I could go on and on, but the first thing to identify, as God did with Israel, is what you are emotionally invested in, your passions. Because if you will follow them, it may very well lead you to your idol and help you get back on track to worshiping God above all other things.

Twelve

What is Your Source of Confidence?

This question relates to pride and identity. I'm not talking about your confidence in a developed skill. I'm asking, when you feel confident among people, what is the source of your confidence? When you're proud of something, what is the *source* of your pride? What gives you identity?

In Hosea 7:10, God says, "*The pride of Israel testifies to his face; yet they do not return to the Lord their God, nor seek him, for all this.*" Israel was off track. They had wandered, spiritually, far out into the wilderness. Notice the phrase, "The pride of Israel" – where Israel was getting their confidence, if you will. And notice, too, that this idea was introduced back in Hosea 5:5. The exact same phrase is used there. "*The pride of Israel testifies to his face; Israel and Ephraim shall stumble in his guilt; Judas also shall stumble with them.*" So it is the pride of Israel that is being identified in this passage. And for Israel, it was their national identity. It was who they were. They were, after all, the people of God. They were the people of David. The Law had been given to *them*. They were the people of Moses. None of that could be said of Assyria, nor Egypt; that couldn't be said of any other nation.

Israel had a national identity, a national confidence that they had come to believe was inherent *in them*. In their minds, they were a superior nation, not because *they belonged to God*, but because He "belonged" to them. As though they had Him in their back pocket – not to rule them, no, no – more like a genie in a bottle, and they were confident because they held the bottle. They'd forgotten who He was, and full of who they were, overly confident in and of themselves. That's what God was illustrating in this passage when He was helping them to discover and identify what their true idol was, what they were really worshiping.

National pride can be a real struggle for Americans. We love our country and it is good and right to be patriotic, but our ultimate allegiance is not to a flag, it's to a cross. And if that statement makes you uncomfortable, you probably just discovered an idol.

But maybe national pride is not your idol, maybe it's a personal pride. So I ask you again, what is it that gives you confidence in life? What makes you feel like you *matter*? What is it that, if the topic comes up, makes you feel like you've gone from loser to Best in Class?

Maybe it's your looks. Are you drop dead gorgeous? Swooningly handsome? Beautiful people often get preferential treatment, so your physical appearance can easily become a priority. Do you pride yourself on your looks?

Do you get your identity from your physical attractiveness? If you came down with a disfiguring skin disease, would you be devastated, feel worthless?

Maybe you're *not* one of the beautiful people. Maybe you're only ordinary looking. Maybe you're actually ugly or disfigured. You still might be obsessed with your lack of physical beauty. Do you *account yourself unworthy* because of your lack of beauty?

Or maybe it's your education that makes you feel like you really matter. Perhaps you went to a better school than most people, or you have *more* education than other people. Do you feel like you're smarter than most of the people you work with, or than others in your family, so you need to instruct them? Are you really proud of your education? Does your confidence derive from it? Would you be devastated if your school were to lose its accreditation? What if the basic premise of whatever field you mastered was debunked, proven invalid by newer information and better technology? Would you feel like a failure?

Or what about money? Maybe you have more money than most people. Does your pride, your confidence come from your financial security? Does your money make you feel powerful? Do you feel like some rules just don't apply to you because you're rich, or that your time is worth more because you have lots of money? Do you feel like you're superior to those around you because you are wealthy? If your accountant embezzled your money and you had to sell your house and possessions to meet your obligations, would you see yourself as a loser?

Don't get me wrong. There is nothing bad about being beautiful, rich, or well educated. There is nothing to apologize for if you are attractive, smart, or wealthy. Those are all good things and almost universally regarded as blessings. But any strength taken to excess becomes a weakness. These questions are to help you determine if your identity is sourced in any of those blessings instead of in God.

And there is a flip side, too. You may be getting your identity from things that are *not* considered blessings. Maybe you have *suffered* more than other people. Maybe, when it comes to the issue of suffering, you feel significant, "I've gone through so much. No one knows how I've suffered. I've faced more difficulty than anybody else. They can't imagine what I've been through." Does being a martyr make you feel, in some way, better than those who haven't suffered the way you have? Is your misfortune your identity? What if God healed you, or your family all returned and loved you lavishly, or you won the lottery? Would you be content, or would you feel like you'd lost your identity?

Maybe you get your identity from the accomplishments of your children, basking in reflected glory. Maybe you feel significant because you're so well-traveled, so experienced.

Maybe you have a wonderful voice. That is an attribute like beauty, highly regarded, easily leading to pride. Is it your source of confidence? Maybe you are a skilled artist, brilliant mathematician, prolific writer, adept pianist. Maybe you have an amazing green thumb. Maybe you are a remarkable yodeler.

You could be/have/do anything, the question is, does your identity, your worth, your confidence come from anything that isn't God Himself?

It may seem unbelievable, but it's possible to make an idol out of a great marriage. Have you thought about that? "I see all these other marriages falling apart, but our marriage, it's strong. It's a great marriage." And that becomes your pride. That becomes what your confidence depends on. And if you're not careful, your healthy marriage, your great marriage can actually be your adultery. I know, mind blown. But you can love your spouse, you can love your good marriage, more than you love God. If you have more confidence in your marriage than you have confidence in Christ, that's an idol. Your good marriage has actually become a form of spiritual adultery.

Let me give you another example from my life just to show how insidious this can be. Often, in my life, it's theology. I can be in a room of people, and we can be talking about sports and I'm thinking, "Yeah, I can carry on a conversation. I like sports. No big deal." We can talk about politics. "Yeah, I've got opinions on that and can talk about that." But then theology is mentioned and something inside perks up. All of a sudden I feel like, "Now I can *own* this conversation. I can shine with these people." When we start talking about theological things, I feel like, "This is something that makes me *matter*." Suddenly, in the conversation with this group of people, I've got a confidence that I can be significant in that moment.

My false god can be my knowledge about the true God.

Sin isn't always blatant or obvious. *Anything* can be made into an idol. My *knowledge* of the true God can become a false god because I'm looking to my *knowledge* to make me feel like I matter. Like I have identity. Like, *now* I'm an important person in the room – as though I didn't matter when I was "only" a child of God. As though being in Christ wasn't enough. Christ is *all* the confidence I need. Being His makes me worthy beyond measure. And this is exactly what the Apostle Paul was talking about in Philippians 3:4.

> *"Though I myself have reason for confidence in the flesh also. If anyone else thinks he has reason for confidence in the flesh, I have more: circumcised on the eighth day, of the people of Israel, of the tribe of Benjamin, a Hebrew of Hebrews; as to the law, a Pharisee; as to zeal, a persecutor of the church; as to righteousness under the law, blameless. But whatever gain I had, I counted as loss for the sake of Christ. Indeed, I count everything as loss because of the surpassing worth of knowing Christ Jesus, my Lord. For his sake, I have suffered the loss of all things and count them as rubbish in order that I might gain Christ and be found in him, not having a righteousness of my own that comes from the law, but that which comes through faith in Christ, the righteousness from God that depends on faith."*

God says in Hosea that Israel's pride testified against them. Their pride was an idol. Their *identity* as The Chosen People of God was their god, instead of *God* being their God. This is subtle, just like my inclination to make my *knowledge* of God into an idol. Think of it this way, if Kate Middleton had married Prince William because she wanted to be a *Windsor*, not because she wanted William, that would be a little like what Israel was doing. Israel valued her position, her title, more than the One who gave it to her. She cared more about having Abraham, David, and Moses in her history than the God who chose them and made them great.

Israel's pride was in who she was, not Whose she was.

If you will follow your pride, follow those things that make you well up with pride when that topic comes up, you will be well on your way to discovering your idol, that thing that you're worshiping more than God. And it will help put you on the road to repentance and worshiping God above all things.

Thirteen

What Expectations Devastate You?

What expectations devastate you if they're not met? Hosea 8:4, *"They made kings, but not through me. They set up princes, but I knew it not. With their silver and gold they made idols for their own destruction."* Think about the imagery here: Israel was taking gold and silver and fashioning idols from them, metal icons that they would look to and worship. And they're doing that in the hope that those idols would solve their problems, help them prosper, or make their crops grow. In other words, they formed the idols hoping that the idols would deliver their hopes and dreams. Israel had expectations that they would get from those idols the things Israel wanted. The gods that those idols represented were promising that if Israel would just worship them, Israel would be taken care of. But the problem is that these gods do not deliver. In fact, they end up causing more problems than they solve. In Israel's case, they wanted salvation, and what they received was destruction. See, here's the reality: Everyone leans up against some kind of wall.

We all have something that we expect will hold us up, will give us what we need, something that we can trust in, we can believe in. But what happens when that wall falls? What happens when you've put all of your hopes and all of your expectations into this wall, and you depend on the promises that you hope to receive from it – and then that wall crumbles? That is exactly what is happening here in Hosea. They fashioned those idols, but what they got was destruction when they had hoped for salvation. Let me read you a quote from C.S. Lewis in *Mere Christianity* that I think really gets at this.

"Most people, if they have really looked into their hearts, would know that they do want, and want acutely, something that cannot be had in this world. There are all sorts of things in this world that offer to give you, but they never quite keep their promise. The longings which arise in us when we first fall in love, or first think of some foreign country, or first take up some subject that really excites us, are longing, which no marriage, no travel, no learning can really satisfy.

Now, I'm not now speaking of that which would be ordinarily called unsuccessful marriages, or holidays, or learned careers. I am speaking of the best possible ones. There was something we grasped at, at that first moment of longing, which fades away in the reality. I think everyone knows what I mean. The wife may be a good wife, and the hotels and the scenery may have been excellent, and chemistry may be an interesting job, but something has evaded us."

We put all of our expectations, all of our hopes that these things will fulfill their promises, will give us what we really want – and the wall doesn't hold us up. What are those things that you're expecting to fulfill those ultimate needs – security, identity, purpose – and yet, time after time, and again and again, they have let you down? There are so many examples of relationships that you have looked to for everything that you need out of life, and they have let you down. You thought being wealthy and having a successful career would ultimately fulfill you. But like Israel, those idols leave you empty. So follow what you are looking toward to solve your promises, to give you those things that you deeply long for, and that will help you discover where your idol truly is so that you can repent of that idol and give your love ultimately to the Lord.

What Do You Fear Losing the Most?

What do you most fear to lose? Hosea 10:5, *"The inhabitants of Samaria tremble for the calf of Beth-aven. Its people mourn for it, and so do its idolatrous priests – those who rejoiced over it and over its glory – for it has departed from them. The thing itself shall be carried to Assyria as tribute to the great king. Ephraim shall be put to shame, and Israel shall be ashamed of his idol."*

Israel is terrified at the thought of losing their idols. God has already warned of judgment to come, that the nation of Assyria is going to descend upon the Northern Kingdom. And the people of Israel are hoping that they can avoid that because if Assyria comes and overtakes Israel, they're going to lose all their idols. The text says they tremble and mourn specifically for the calf in Samaria. Baal is often represented as a bull or calf, and Israel was terrified that if Assyria invaded Israel, they would lose their idol, and they could not imagine life without their idol. It is like a drug user. If you know somebody who's on drugs, or if you have been around people like that, you know that they hardly think about anything else. It's all they want. They cannot imagine a scenario where they won't get another high. They can't fathom a future without that drug, and they're terrified at the possibility of losing it.

What is that for you? What is that thing in your life that you would be devastated if you lost? That your life almost would be not worth living if you didn't have? It could be a spouse, or a child, or your money, health, reputation – it could be a host of things. For Israel, it was their idol, so Israel was in a panic. trembling at the thought of losing that idol. And an idol doesn't have to be something horrid like Baal.

So really think about this. You can't study the book of Hosea and not identify your idol; that is what this book is about, because we are like Gomer, going after other lovers. So, what are those other lovers in your life? What are those passions that burn out of control? What is the pride that gives you your identity, that is the source of confidence for you? What promises are you looking for other things to fulfill? And what causes you panic at the thought of losing? This is why God gave us these verses, in order for us to identify our idol. He gave us this because He wants us to turn back to Him. Why? Because God wants you to be where you belong, and where you belong is with Him, just like Israel. In this passage, God is exposing these things in Israel's life because He wants His wayward wife to come back into His arms.

In fact, notice how this section ends. Hosea 10:12, "*Sow for yourselves righteousness; reap steadfast love; break up your fallow ground, for it is the time to seek the Lord, that he may come and rain righteousness upon you.*" What an amazing verse that is. He is saying it is time to seek the Lord. It is time to recalculate your life and get on the right path. But to do that, you've got to identify your idol. You've got to call out what it is that you've been worshiping instead of God. And when you do that, when you repent and you return to Him, what's going to be waiting for you, an angry, vengeful husband? No. A silent, won't-even-speak-to-you husband? No. What's waiting for you is a God who wants to rain righteousness upon you. He can't wait for you to return. He welcomes His wayward wife back into His arms.

And so if you're like Albert and Rita and you've gone off the map spiritually, will you return to the right path? Will you turn from your idols, and will you turn to God? If you will, He is waiting to rain righteousness on you. And how do we know that that is true? How do we know that Hosea 10:12 is true? Because God sent His Son into the world with specific directions, and Jesus never once veered off course until He reached the final destination of the cross and the empty tomb. And He did that because God so loved the world. You see, the good news of the gospel is that Jesus never got lost. So no matter how lost you may be, you are never beyond the bounds of His love.

Fourteen

He Has It Worse

The year that Lisa turned 30 was the year she fell in love. At first, that sense of love gave her hope. It gave her enjoyment in life. There was just one huge problem. The man she loved did not love her. Here is how Lisa describes this season in her life. She wrote:

> "I woke up at dawn. I wanted to hold onto the blankness of sleep, but thoughts of him quickly crept into my mind. It had been a long time since I had thought of anything but him. I spent hours, days, weeks, months, imagining my future with him, but there would be no future together. He wasn't with me, not in that moment and not in the next. No, he was asleep in his own bed in his ninth-floor apartment, a 10-minute walk across town that morning, I decided to pay him a visit.

I stood there in the lobby in front of the security door. I rummaged through my purse like a tenant trying to find her key. Someone happened to walk out and, without asking me any questions, let me inside. I took the elevator to the ninth floor.

I knocked softly at first, but he didn't answer. My knocking continued, getting a little louder with each knock. Eventually the knocking got so loud the neighbor came out to see if it was someone at his door. The neighbor assumed I had the right to be there, and I clung to that assumption, as well.

Finally, after several rounds of knocking, I decided on a different approach. I went up on the rooftop. It was a chilly, windy November morning and the gray wind whipped around me. The rooftop reminded me of those summer nights that he and I spent together looking into the sky sipping bourbon.

After a few minutes passed, I went back down and continued knocking. After all, who would reject this kind of desire? Who would turn away from this kind of love? Isn't this what people dream of? And just as I was thinking this, the door opened, there stood the love of my life, but the words he spoke shattered my heart.

'Lisa, leave before I call the cops.'

That's when I finally realized the truth. The truth I had suppressed for some time: I was in love with a man who didn't love me back.

Those words come from Lisa Phillips in her book *Unrequited*, and she recounts a true story of love and obsession with a man whom she desperately wanted to be with, that she wanted to be with more than anything, but a man who did not want to be with her. Let me ask you this. Have you ever wanted something badly – I mean *really*, **really** *wanted*, and yet that desire was not reciprocated, the desired one did not want you the same way? Maybe, like Lisa, you were in love with someone who didn't love you. Or maybe you really wanted to work for that company, but they had no interest in hiring you. Or you urgently wanted to go to that particular school, but they refused to accept you. Or you desperately wanted the love of your father, but you never received that from him. Maybe you really wanted to reconcile a relationship, but they wanted nothing to do with you.

There's a scene from the 2011 movie, *Warrior*, that illustrates this:

SON: *Aw, Forget it. Yeah, I'll tell you part of the reason. Part of the reason I stuck around because I thought I'd finally get you all to myself, but you didn't have any interest in training me. You had Tommy, he was the one.*

FATHER: *Brendon, I was a drunk. I mean, you know – I'm sorry.*

SON: *No, forget it. You're always a front runner. Never had any interest in underdogs. But I was your son.*

FATHER: *You are my son, Brendan.*

SON: *No, I'm not.*

FATHER: *Yeah, you are. I just – I'm just asking you if you can find a little bit of space in your heart and forgive me a little bit.*

SON: *Yeah, I have forgave you.*

FATHER:	*Okay –*
SON:	*But I do not trust you.*
FATHER:	*Aw –*
SON:	*Listen, tell Tommy, if he wants to see me, this is where I am. [TURNS AWAY]*
FATHER:	*Okay, but – they're not different things. You gotta trust to forgive*
SON:	*'Bye, Pop. [OPENS DOOR REVEALING A WOMAN AND CHILD]*
FATHER:	*Oh, my God. Is that Emily? She's grown! Brendon? Is that Rosie – [SON STEPS INSIDE]*
LITTLE GIRL:	*Daddy, who is that?*
SON:	*That's a nice old man. [CLOSING DOOR]*
FATHER:	*C'mon. How about a cup of coffee – [DOOR CLICKS SHUT]*

Most of us can relate to that feeling of wanting something, wanting someone, and yet not having that desire returned the same way. But have you ever stopped to think about the fact that that is exactly how God feels regarding *you*? That God desires you more than you desire Him? That when it comes to your relationship with God, He has it worse than you do? Does that seem odd to you? Is that a thought you've ever had about God? Well, that is exactly what Hosea 7:13 teaches us. Focus specifically on the last part of the verse. *"Woe to them, for they have strayed from me! Destruction to them, for they have rebelled against me! I would redeem them, but they speak lies against me.*

I Would Redeem Them

Let's break that last phrase down, "*I would redeem them.*" What was God saying about His people? He was saying, "I want to save them. I want to be in relationship with them. I want to purchase them to myself. I do not want them worshiping other gods. I want them to worship me alone so that they will be full of enjoyment and satisfaction. I want them because I love them." He really loves his people. He wants to redeem His people. And His love is not based on any goodness within *them*. It is not based on anything that they have done. It is purely based on who *He* is. We looked at Hosea 11:8 earlier, when God said, "*How can I give you up, O Ephraim? How can I hand you over, O Israel? How can I make you like Admah? How can I treat you like Zeboim* [cities destroyed along with Sodom and Gomorrah]? *My heart recoils within me; my compassion grows warm and tender. I will not execute my burning anger; I will not again destroy Ephraim; for I am God and not a man.*" [Emphasis mine]

The love of God is based on *God*, not on our goodness. God loves this way because that's how God loves. He wants his people. He loves his people. He is a desiring God. God desires to be in relationship with the people He loves. Just like Gomer. Even though she was a whore, Hosea loved her and wanted to be with her. And remember, Hosea and Gomer were a living metaphor of God and His people. In our text in Hosea 7:13, God said, "*I would redeem them,*" I want them, I love them. The one preventing the full experience of God's love was not God. It was Israel.

It isn't God who prevents us from feeling His love. We prevent it.

It was not God who was keeping Israel from the full experience of His love. He wanted to redeem them; the issue was with Israel. God's purpose was clear, the reluctance in that relationship was not coming from God, it was coming from the people of God. God reached out; it was His people who turned away and ran off to all their lovers, their idols. So, God had it worse in that relationship. He loved them more than they loved Him. He desired them more than they desired Him. He wanted to redeem them, but they spoke lies against him.

Now, let's be honest, I know what you're thinking. Doesn't this seem a little pathetic to you? Almost like a high school relationship where the guy is, like, a pathetic loser? I mean, is this really the way God – the sovereign God of the universe – is acting towards His people? I mean, after all, what would you say about a man who gets rejected over and over, cheated on over and over, and then when his wife comes to him for something, not only does he forgive her, he gives her what she wants, *and* he wants to romance her. I'm sure we'd all call that guy pathetic. What a pathetic loser who just takes that, over and over and over again. And yet – that is the story of Hosea. That is exactly what the book of Hosea teaches. Gomer, representing Israel, repeatedly breaks her vows, while Hosea, representing God, buys her back without conditions. Why? Because he loves her. That's the story of Hosea and it's outrageous. It's absolutely outrageous, but such is the love of God.

The love of God is not pathetic, the love of God is *permanent*.

God's love is not weak or limp-wristed. It is permanent. It's a love that will not let you go. It's a love that is not going anywhere. It is a love that will not forsake you no matter how many times you forsake God. You see, the great news of unconditional love is this: It has no conditions. God's love is not pathetic, it is just *so* strong and so all-encompassing that we can't even comprehend it. It's like a primitive looking at the prairie that stretches, *flat as flat*, all the way to the horizon in every direction while being told that the Earth is round like a ball. It's incomprehensible, It's contrary to all of your senses. However, if you trust the speaker, it's not unbelievable.

Here's the better question – what is wrong with us? As Lisa asked in that opening story, who would reject this kind of desire? Who would turn away from this kind of love? Why do we settle for bad lovers? Why do we reject the very love that would make us whole? Why do we turn from the very thing that would satisfy us the most? Let's look at what God said next, "But they speak lies against me." I would redeem them. I desire them. I love them. I want them. I want to purchase them – but they speak lies against me.

But They Speak Lies Against Me

The reason Israel rejected God and God's redeeming love was because she believed lies about God. Stop and think about that for just a moment because we do the same. The reason you don't want God the way He wants you is because there are things you believe about God that aren't true. You have a false notion of who God is and what He is like, and because you believe that false notion of what God is like, you don't go to Him, you don't love Him, and instead you run after other things and you have other lovers. If you saw God rightly, you would desire God fully.

If Israel had seen God rightly, they would have clung to Him. God loved His people. God wanted to be with His people. He said, "I would redeem them." The problem was *their* reluctance, *their* rejection. And why were they rejecting God's love and His redemption? Because they believed lies. They didn't have a full understanding of who God is. Their beliefs about God weren't accurate. If they had truly known Him, they couldn't help but want Him, and love Him, and make Him the chief object of their hearts. This is deeply significant; there is a lot on the line here for us. What are the lies that *we* believe about God that keep us from experiencing His love?

Fifteen

The Myths of Our Unbelief

Hosea 7:13 doesn't tell us what the lies are, nor do the verses that follow. When the text says, *"But they speak lies against me,"* you might expect a litany of what those lies are, but it just continues describing what Israel was doing. So you're left to ask, "Well, what were these lies that Israel believed about God or spoke about God?" When doing a critical analysis of a text, we want to be faithful to the scripture. So if the verse doesn't *tell* you what the lies are, the next step would be to ask if there is anything in the totality of the book that might help us understand what these lies are? In other words, what is the book of Hosea about? What was Israel doing from which we might understand where the lies originated?

Here is a quick review of the main issue in the book of Hosea. See if you can figure out what is going on.

1. Hosea 1:2, When the Lord first spoke through Hosea, the Lord said to him, *"Go take yourself a wife of whoredom and have children of whoredom, for the land commits great whoredom by forsaking the Lord."*

2. Hosea 2:13, *"I will punish her for the feast of the Baals when she burned offerings to them and adorned herself with her ring and jewelry and went after her lovers and forgot me."*

3. Hosea 3:1, *"The Lord said to me, 'Go again, love a woman who is loved by another man and is an adulteress, even as the Lord loves the children of Israel, though they turn to other gods.'"*

4. Hosea 4:17, *"Ephraim is joined to idols; leave him alone. When their drink is gone, they give themselves to whoring."*

5. Hosea 5:3, *"I know Ephraim and Israel is not hidden from me; for now, O Ephraim, you have played the whore; Israel is defiled. Their deeds do not permit them to return to their God. For the spirit of whoredom is within them, and they do not know the Lord."*

6. Hosea 6:10, *"In the house of Israel I have seen a horrible thing. Ephraim's whoredom is there; Israel is defiled."*

7. Hosea 7:4, *"They are all adulterers; they are like a heated oven whose baker ceases to stir the fire."*

8. Hosea 8:9, *"For they have gone up to Assyria, a wild donkey wandering alone; Ephraim has hired lovers."*

9. Hosea 9:1, "*Rejoice not, O Israel! Exult not like the peoples; for you have played the whore, forsaking your God. You have loved a prostitute's wages on all threshing floors.*"

That's a lot, I know, but I laid out every one of those verses so that you would realize it doesn't take a seminary degree to figure out what the issue is. The primary issue, the ultimate issue in the book of Hosea is the issue of idolatry, loving other things more than you love God. So now we have a vital question to ask. What is it about our idolatry that speaks lies about God?

"God's Acceptance is Based on My Performance."

We saw earlier that Israel was worshiping God the same way they worshiped Baal. They were even calling God by Baal's name. God said, "*No longer will you call me Baal.*" In other words, they were worshiping God the same way they were worshiping the false gods. Well, how are *any* other gods worshipped? You perform. You do what makes the gods happy. In return, they promise to make *you* happy. The lie that we believe – and we learn it from our idols – is that God's acceptance of us is based on *what we do*. Instead of love, God's acceptance is based on law. This is a lie. This is how the lie works: you perform for God. You try to be the best you can be for God. You try to live up to the law for God. You try to be as religious as you can be for God. You do everything you can to have a squeaky-clean life, and you perform to the point of exhaustion. You are spiritually spent. You have done the best that you possibly could, and you know that even your best was filthy rags. And do you know what you do then? You stop desiring God. You stop going to God because you think, "What's the point? It's never enough."

I know this because I've done it myself. When I was in high school I got to the point where it was feeling like my whole Christianity was based on what I did for God, and I crashed and burned. I reached a point when I said, "God, I don't want to do this anymore. I'm just done with You because whatever I do, it's never enough. I try to be the best person I can be, and yet this stuff happens. I don't want to do this anymore." And in that moment, it was like the Spirit of God said, "Finally. It's about time you stop thinking that this is about your performance."

But that's what our idols teach us because in the rest of life we're performing to keep our idols happy. So we think the same thing must be true about God when it is actually a lie that keeps us from Him. What was God trying to teach His people? Hosea 6:6, "*I desire steadfast love and not sacrifice, the knowledge of God rather than burnt offerings.*" See, the point of the Law – all of the instructions to do this, and don't do that, and perform these sacrifices – the point of the Law was to prove that God's acceptance of you could only be a matter of love, it could never be based on the Law. Do you know why? Because you suck at keeping the Law. You're terrible at keeping the Law. You fall short a whole lot more than you ever live up. This was the whole reason why God gave the Law, to prove to you that, unlike for your idols, you don't have to perform for Him because your relationship is based on His love, not the Law.

Idolatry teaches us a lie about God. And if we believe that lie, namely that my acceptance is based on my performance, then I'm eventually going to burn out and say, "Forget this. I don't want to come to You anymore because it doesn't work." But when you start to realize that your acceptance is based on His performance, not yours, only then will you be truly free to come to Him and make Him the object of your love.

"God is Not Sufficient For My Needs."

As we've seen, the reason why Israel had turned, specifically, to Baal was for provision. It was because Israel had come to believe that God was not sufficient to give them what they needed. They had been convinced that they needed the other gods if they were ever going to get the good life they wanted. Remember Hosea 2:5? "*For their mother has played the whore; she who conceived them has acted shamefully. For she said, 'I will go after my lovers,* [the idol worship] *who give me my bread and my water and my wool and my flax and my oil and my drink.*" Right here is the lie. The idols teach you that, *in addition to God,* you need other things to have the good life, to enjoy life. I need God + _____, in order for my life to be fulfilled. The idol doesn't say, "You don't need God," not at first. But, eventually, your love for that idol is going to surpass your love for God and you'll stop going to Him at all. How do I know that? It's what Jesus said: "You can't serve two masters." Your idol doesn't want you to believe you can enjoy life without it.

You see the draw of idolatry is the promise that it will give you something that, in reality, only God can give you. And what happens is that it becomes your god and your idol because you believe that God alone is not enough. "I need this to give me my flax, and my oil, and my wool, and my bread, and my water. I need something that God won't give." And so you have two masters. You have two gods, or three, or six, or whatever. And what is inevitably going to happen is that these false gods will squeeze out the true God and you won't go to Him anymore. You won't desire Him anymore. "*I would redeem them, but they speak lies against me.*"

"My Sin is Too Great For God's Love."

In Hosea 5:13, when Israel realized her sin and what a mess she had made, rather than turning to God in repentance, she ran to Assyria, hoping that the king of Assyria would be able to cure her problem, would be able to heal her. Remember that, because God loved her, He warned her that Assyria would destroy her if she didn't come back to God for pardon. All she had to do was to come back to Him for cleansing. But instead, she ran straight to the Assyrian king to try to make some deal with him, as though she could somehow circumvent God's plan! This is further proof that Israel believed God was not powerful enough to do what was needful. And it also shows how little they knew their God. How deeply the lies had gone.

How often do *we* take our issues, the troubles that we're dealing with, to other people instead of God because we don't really think that God could love someone who is struggling with *that*? We don't really think that God could love someone who has *done that*, whatever "that" is. In a lot of ways, we're like the prodigal son. Do you remember that story in Luke 15 when the prodigal son convinced himself that there was no possible way he could ever be received back as a son if he were to return to the father? That the best he could be was a hired slave. That was the thinking of the prodigal. And we think the same way. "After what I've done, there's no way I can go to God, so I've got to go to something else." It looks like this. We sin, and we tell ourselves that since God would never receive us as a son or daughter *now*, we'll go to something that will: the bottle, a best friend, money, food, whatever, because our idols have convinced us of the lie that they will accept us and make us feel good even when God will not.

This fact is so powerful, so important for us to receive. "*I would redeem them, but they speak lies.*" All of these lies – My relationship is based on performance, God alone is not enough, My sin is too bad for God to love me– These are lies we've learned from our idolatry, and they keep us from desiring God, keep us from enjoying God and resting in His love.

The Motivation of Our Unbelief

What motivates us to believe these lies in the first place? One motivation is that we *want* to believe the lies. We want to believe that our relationship is based on performance, that God could never love someone who has done what I've done, that He's not sufficient. I think that there's a sense within us that wants to believe that these things are true. And why is that so? Because if we believe the truth that God's love is unconditional and that He really loves us and really desires us, this would cost us at least two things.

Sixteen

We Lose All Grounds For Boasting

The first thing God's unconditional love would take from us is any basis for boasting. If God's love is not based on our performance, if it is based on Him alone, if it is unconditional, then we cannot take credit for anything. And in a performance-based culture like ours, the last thing that we want is to give up our good showing. We would never actually *call* it boasting, but we want others to see that we're performing well. Pharisees would rather perform than admit that they need redemption. I'd rather be distant from God than admit I'm desperate for God. So what happens? We hold onto the lie of the Law at the expense of experiencing His love. *We* hold onto the Law, God doesn't crush us under it. It has got to be about *my* performance. Even though it is a lie, I want to believe it because I don't want to give up my boasting, give up my audience.

I want this, in some way, to be about me. At my core, I am a Pharisee. *I don't need to be purchased. It's about performing.* So we hold onto the lie because we don't want to believe the truth. We don't really want to believe the unconditional love of God because that would mean we couldn't take credit for anything.

We Lose All Grounds For Excuses

A second motivation for accepting lies is that if we really believe in the unconditional love of God, we lose all grounds for excuses. If we believe the lie that God is not for us, then why should we be for Him? And notice this. If we can convince ourselves that God's love for us is conditional, then our love for Him can be conditional, as well. If I can convince myself that the unconditional love of God cannot be true, it's got to be based on conditions, then my love for Him can be based on conditions, too. Imagine we're in the Garden of Eden. If I believe that God is not for me, well, then I can excuse my eating of the fruit. So what happens is that instead of believing in the truth of the unconditional love of God, I hold onto the lie to justify my own lack of love. But if God's love is unconditional, then there is no excuse for refusing to go to Him no matter how bad my sin may be. If I accept that God's love for me is unconditional, not only do I have no grounds for boasting, I also have no grounds for excuses.

God wants to redeem his people. "*I would redeem them,*" that's what the verse says, "*but they speak lies against me.*" That is, there are lies. There are false notions about God that we learned from our idols that keep us from going to

Him. They keep us reluctant to enjoy Him fully. But why? Because, deep down, we don't want to truly believe it is unconditional, for once we let go of that lie that God's love is conditional and believe the truth that God's love is unconditional, you and I can't boast about a thing and you and I have no excuses anymore because there is nothing keeping you "from the love of God that is in Christ Jesus." [Romans 8:1]

God loves us more than we love Him. Why? God pursues us; He desires us more than we desire Him. Why? Because we believe lies that we learn from our idols about Him and they keep us from going to Him. And we would rather keep it that way because believing the lie justifies our sin, the sin of not going to Him. My hope is that you're going to stop believing those lies about God, and that you're going to believe the truth of His love. Then you will go to Him fully and completely, and there will be no "but" of Hosea 7:13. Instead, it will be "I would redeem them – and they believe my truth."

So, what is the absolute, undeniable truth that is found in this book of Hosea? It is this: God loves you. "*I would redeem them.*" God wants to redeem a prostitute. God loves you in all of your waywardness and all of your idol worship. God still desires you, He still wants you. You may rationalize this and explain that – but stop for a moment. Don't block what your heart needs because of what your mind thinks. I'm not suggesting that we shouldn't renew our minds. I'm just telling you to stop overanalyzing what you've done and who you've been in your past and just accept what the word says, which is, "I want to redeem them. I love them. I desire my people. I want to be in relationship with them." He loves you. Period.

Whatever you've done, He desires you and wants you, regardless of what you think reality is. Because the truth is that what *God* says about reality *is* reality, not what you think reality is. It's like this, imagine a man dealing with Parkinson's and experiencing frequent hallucinations, but he's aware that these hallucinations are happening. One day he turns to his daughter and asks, "Is there a horse standing in the middle of the room?" And she says, "No, Dad, there is no horse standing in the middle of the room." The Dad accepts that reality. He is *looking at* the horse, but he accepts that reality, that there is no horse standing in the middle of the room, because he understands that, due to his condition, his perception of reality isn't accurate.

The reality at times *appears* to be that God could never love you, but you don't get to define reality because your sin has made you delusional. What you need is not to overthink and overanalyze what you've done, or who you are, or the character and nature of God. God's word says, "I love you." Accept that reality because God said it. Regardless of what you think or what you feel, God says to his people, "I would redeem you. I desire you. I want you to be mine." Accept this. You committed to God, then you broke your vows and you ran off to other lovers, and you played religious games while your heart did not love him. And yet God's word is still saying to you today, "Come to me. I want to be with you. I will love you unconditionally." Accept and embrace that that is truth regardless of whatever lie you have believed.

And if the Book of Hosea is not enough, the cross certainly is because the cross is the proof of what Hosea teaches us. Let Romans 5:8 sink deeply into your heart and mind, "*But God shows his love for us in that while we were still sinners, Christ died for us.*" Notice the verb tenses in that verse. "God shows," that is present tense, right now in this moment God is showing you something, He is demonstrating something. And what is He showing you? He's showing you His love for sinners, people who have repeatedly fallen short like Gomer. So how is He *now* showing you that He loves you, a *sinner*? "Christ *died* for us." Past tense. There is a past event, the death of Jesus Christ, that secures a present reality, namely, the proof that God desires you today. There is a past event, the crucifixion of Jesus Christ that demonstrates to you that today, present tense, you are loved and desired by God. That's the gospel. That is what we find in Jesus Christ. And it is based on absolutely nothing that you have done, it is based entirely on what Christ has done for you. And the moment that you actually start to believe that, God will become the chief object of your desire. You will cherish Him as the lover of your soul, the one you desire more than anything else.

So Lisa Phillips' story is not just her story. It is the story of the book of Hosea. It is the story of the gospel. It is the story of the God who desires you, though you may not desire Him, who is faithful to you, though you're not always faithful to Him, who will not walk away from you, even though you walk away from Him. It is the story of the One who, according to Revelation 3:20, stands at the door and knocks. So maybe you should ask yourself the same thing Lisa asked herself, Who would reject this kind of desire? Who would turn away from this kind of love? Listen up, wayward wife. Listen up, prodigal son, it is time for you to stop believing the lies and start believing the truth of God: He has an outrageous love for you.

Seventeen

From Facts to Feelings

It was around this time last year that I was admitted to the hospital. After months of being so short of breath I could barely walk a few steps without gasping for air, my lungs and heart were being crushed by a buildup of fluid. I had an aneurysm in my lung that was bleeding, threatening to rupture with fatal consequences. I was malnourished and dangerously thin. My doctor didn't mince words. It was 6:30 a.m. when he entered the room, waking me from a restless sleep, standing over me while I lay in bed.

He said, "I'm afraid you may never leave the hospital. You're dying."

My first reaction was disbelief. I tried to argue with him. "I would be in intensive care if I was dying. A few months ago, my cancer had been deemed stable. Sure, I wasn't feeling great, but how could I be dying?"

The doctor then said, "I know this must be hard to hear of someone your age."

I asked him about the aneurysm. "Are they still going to try to fix it?"

And the doctor replied, "To be honest, if it ruptures, it'll be a blessing in disguise because, at least, it will be quick."

Wait. So not only am I dying, I am going to die a slow and painful death.

After the doctor left, I wondered what I should do now that I was dying. Everything suddenly felt different even though nothing had changed. I debated as to whether or not to call my parents and relay the news over the phone or wait until I would see them in person. But when I called my mom, I couldn't contain it. My family arrived at the hospital within the hour, and we sat in silence, crying, trying to absorb it all.

That real life experience of a young man is an example of what Dr. Nessa Coyle calls the existential slap: That moment when a dying person first comprehends, on a gut level, that death is imminent. Dr. Coyle is a nurse practitioner who specializes in end-of-life care at MSK Cancer Center in New York. She says, "The existential slap is when the usual habit of allowing thoughts of death to remain in the background is now impossible, death can no longer be denied." Dr. Coyle has observed that when their doctor tells them that their illness is terminal, it triggers a personal crisis in many patients.

Virginia Lee, another medical professional who specializes in advanced cancer care, writes, "Most people recognize at an intellectual level that death is inevitable. But in western culture, we think we're going to live forever. My patients often tell me they thought of death as something that happened to other people until they received the diagnosis."

Have you ever experienced an existential slap? Not necessarily told that you're dying, but that moment when what you *knew* as fact became real, *felt*. We all know intellectually or factually that we're going to die. But in that moment when you're told that death is imminent, you feel that slap, and what was merely fact before becomes felt. My guess is that we've all experienced that in some way. For instance, maybe you *knew* that you weren't performing well at the job, but it wasn't until the day you were called into the office and told you were fired, that you *felt* it. Or maybe you knew that your grades weren't good, but it wasn't until the final scores were posted that you felt the slap. Or you knew the relationship wasn't going well, but it wasn't until she said, "We need to talk," that you felt it. The existential slap can be a positive experience, too. You'd always expected to have kids one day, but it wasn't until you saw him the first time that you felt the slap. Or you knew, intellectually, about love, but it wasn't until you met *her*.......*slap!*

Most adults, in one way or the other, have felt that existential slap, that moment in life when what you only knew "theoretically" became something you could feel. And the same thing happens to us spiritually in different seasons throughout our walk with God, when things that we know theologically, factually, intellectually, suddenly become real, we feel it "in our bones." We see the facts in a completely new way, and it causes what is often called a paradigm shift. Life is different, now, than it was a moment ago.

This existential slap is what the book of Hosea is meant to administer to us regarding the love of God. That is, we know John 3:16, we've sung "Jesus loves me, this I know" ever since we were kids, and we've heard countless sermons on the love of God – and yet we walk away unmoved. We know that it's true, we've seen evidence that it's true, but we haven't had that slap of realization that it's true for *me* – that God truly, personally, and intimately loves *me* with no strings attached, no conditions. I am simply loved. What tells me that this is the purpose of the book of Hosea? The language used.

Hosea uses language that is shocking, and intense, and alarming. In fact, such language may have made it difficult for you to read this book. This is not just some factual dissertation on the love of God. The language of Hosea is direct and brutally honest, it doesn't include the euphemisms or innuendos of polite conversation. It tells the stark, unvarnished truth about us, and then the brilliant, unfiltered truth about Him. Let me give you an example. If I were to say to you, "You're a sinner, but God loves you," that may impact you a little bit, but that doesn't affect you like it would if I said, "You are a spiritual whore." Now I've got your attention. Now you're emotionally engaged. You may be deeply offended – but with a little explanation, a little thought, you come to realize the truth of it. You *are* a spiritual whore, just as I am. We have repeatedly committed spiritual adultery by loving other things more than we love God.

It is quite possible that you have never understood God's definition of *sin*. Maybe you have always thought of sin as things you *did*: Stealing, killing, or a prideful heart. Maybe you never realized that those specific actions that God called out in the Ten Commandments were really only *symptoms* of sin. Sin is first internal; it is born in us and comes from the heart. Sin is the result of not loving God with all of your soul, mind, and strength. Perhaps you have thought of the first commandment, "You shall have no other gods before Me," as an outdated, irrelevant rule – after all, civilized folks haven't gotten on their knees in front of gods of wood or stone in centuries, right? But that first commandment is the one that will make all of the others come quite naturally. Once you know that not loving God with your whole heart is *the* sin that leads to all others, you'll quickly realize that almost everything you do is idolatry. Hosea is right, we *are* whores. **SLAP** It all just got real.

And then, with a terribly *real* understanding of just how wayward you have been, you turn your eyes in dismay to God, and find Him not stern and condemning, not vengeful and cynical, but *eager* to redeem you, romance you, and renew His covenant with you. That is powerful. That is transformational. Then you realize that, not only did you not understand what sin is, you didn't even have a *clue* about God's love. The scripture says in I John 4:7 that God is Love, not that God has love for us, or that He has many attributes among which is love – God *is* Love. The best love we've ever experienced in our lives is but a spark compared to the SUN of God's love, which is God Himself. Not a weak and squishy sentimentality that needs your affection, but a passionate desire for relationship with you, His creature.

Look again at Hosea 2:14, it says, *Therefore, behold, I will allure her, I'll bring her into the wilderness and speak tenderly to her. And there I'll give her vineyards and make the Valley of Achor* [affliction], *a valley of hope. And there she shall answer as in the days of her youth, as at the time when she came out of the land of Egypt.*" Israel had played the whore with other gods, and this was God's response. You have played the whore with other, more modern gods – His response is the same. You can *feel* that. Hosea is, I believe, that existential slap of the reality of our sin, and the mind-boggling reality of God's love, to move us from fact to feeling.

So, let's follow the text in Hosea that shows the contrast between what Israel deserved (which we also deserve) and God's attitude about what they would get, and why.

Eighteen

The Reasons Why We Should <u>Not</u> Be Loved By God

There are so many reasons why God should not love us, and Israel exhibits all of them. We've seen Israel's sin and rebellion repeated over and over in earlier chapters, so in Hosea 12 it's no surprise to see it on display again. I'm not going to go over the specifics verse by verse this time. Instead I'm going to lump them into three buckets, or categories of sin to show the reasons why a holy God should *not* love Israel, which is also why God should not love us.

Acts of Sin

Israel committed acts of sin against God. More specifically, Israel had been breaking the Ten Commandments they'd vowed to obey. We noted this earlier, but we'll take a look at just a few examples.

Hosea 11:12 says, *"Ephraim has surrounded me with lies, and the house of Israel with deceit."* As we've seen before, this is speaking of idolatry, not of bearing false witness against their neighbor (of course, they'll get to that, too). Idolatry is all about lies, the gods are lies, they lie about the True God, and Israel had put those false gods between them and Yahweh. In other words, God was saying, "Israel, your idol worship is ever before me. It is constantly present. You are always worshiping other things." So, that was the first commandment they had broken.

Hosea 12:1, *"Ephraim feeds on the wind and pursues the east wind all day long; they multiply falsehood and violence."* I told you they'd get to that. They broke the ninth commandment, not to bear false witness, not to lie.

Hosea 12:7, *"A merchant in whose hands are false balances, he loves to oppress."* They were stealing, cheating people. That violated the eighth commandment.

Hosea 13:2a, *"And now they sin more and more and make for themselves metal images, idols skillfully made of their silver, all of them the work of craftsmen."* They violated the second commandment, not to make any graven images.

Hosea 13:2b, *"It is said of them, 'Those who offer human sacrifice kiss calves.'"* They violated the sixth commandment, do not murder.

You get the point, every other verse shows them breaking another commandment, vows that they had promised to keep. There were specific acts of sin taking place in the nation of Israel. They were repeatedly breaking the law; and the wages of sin, the payment for sin, is death. If you had a business, what would you do with an employee who was always late, didn't do his duties, advertised for your competition, and stole your money? What wages would they have earned? God didn't owe Israel anything. By rights, God should have washed His hands of them. One reason Israel did not deserve God's love was her acts of sin. She didn't deserve God's love because she repeatedly broke the law.

Attitude of Self-Righteousness

This one is hard to believe. Hosea 8:1,2, *"Set the trumpet to your lips! One like a vulture is over the house of the Lord because they have transgressed my covenant and rebelled against my law. To me they cry, 'My God, we–Israel–know you.'"* So they repeatedly broke the law of God, and yet when the vulture shows up, they're like this, "Who, me? Who? What? Oh, that's no big deal, right? I mean we're good. We know you. We're on good terms with you, right?" And you also see it in Hosea 12:8, *"Ephraim has said, 'Ah, but I am rich; I have found wealth for myself; in all my labors they cannot find in me iniquity or sin."* Anyone would ask, "Are you out of your mind?" We just read how many verses about their violations of the commandments they'd vowed to keep, and yet they said, "God, we're good, right? We know You, we're on good terms. You can't find any iniquity or sin in us." It's crazy, is it not? But they had convinced themselves that they were okay.

Now you might say, how in the world is that possible? How could they break the commandments that consistently for that long, and then sit there and say, "Aw, you can't find any iniquity in me"? The answer is actually found in that same verse, one word: wealthy. Prosperity. Israel had prospered, they'd become wealthy, life was good. And because they had come to believe lies about God, they didn't believe that He'd let them prosper if He was unhappy with them. So that's how they could break God's law and still justify it, because they looked at their prosperity and thought, "God's blessing me, I must be doing something right." Sound familiar? Instead of their prosperity leading Israel to be grateful to their gracious and forbearing God, it created self-righteousness in their hearts, so they didn't acknowledge their sin.

This is an important lesson for us to learn. Israel justified their law-breaking because of their life blessing. We do this, too. It's so easy to read the wrong meaning into circumstances: bad circumstances mean someone did something wrong, or that God is unhappy with you, while good circumstances mean someone did something right, God is happy with you. God doesn't work that way. Blessings come from God by His grace, not our goodness. We do not have the things we have because we are good. We have them because God is gracious. But Israel forgot that and became self-righteous. So, not only did Israel break all of the commandments that they had vowed to do, but they also patted themselves on the back for their obvious good behavior! If there was a prize for Lack of Self-Awareness, Israel would have won it.

Authority of Self

In spite of 1500 years of history with Yahweh, Hosea tells us that Israel had forgotten God. Let me show you this in Hosea 13:5,6. *"It was I who knew you in the wilderness, in the land of drought; but when they had grazed, they became full, they were filled and their heart was lifted up; therefore, they forgot me."* Earlier we talked about how Israel had no knowledge of God and how that didn't mean that they had become atheists. It didn't mean that they suddenly didn't know that God existed or didn't know who He was. That's not what God meant here. He meant they were not recognizing God's authority in their life. "Forgetting God" is not becoming an atheist, it is rejecting His authority. Intellectually, you know there is a God, but functionally, you live like He doesn't exist, or like He's not paying attention. Or you pick and choose the parts of God you want, and "forget" the rest. Even though God had created them, called them to be His People, and made covenant with them, Israel rejected His authority to tell them how to live their lives.

So, there are just three reasons why God should *not* love a wayward people. If I were a celestial lawyer, this case would be a slam dunk. I can make a very compelling case for why God should *not* love Israel and, quite frankly, why He should not love *us*. Look at our acts of sin, look at our attitude of self-righteousness, and look at our refusal to recognize His authority and, instead, to view ourselves as an authority. And yet....

Nineteen

The Reality Is That We Are Loved By God

Even with all of the acts of sin, the attitude of self-righteousness, and the rejection of His authority, God still, amazingly and outrageously, professes His love for His people. Hosea 12:2, *"The Lord has an indictment against Judah and will punish Jacob according to his ways; He will repay him according to his deeds. in the womb he took his brother by the heel, and in his manhood he strove with God."* You may be thinking, "What in the world is that about?" It is about a little Jewish history. Hosea is going to draw a parallel with a person in the Old Testament by the name of Jacob.

Hosea is drawing a comparison between Israel in her current state in the book of Hosea and Jacob from the book of Genesis. And what do we know about Jacob? Well, we know that Jacob was not a good man at all. Jacob was a deceiver. He came out of the womb fighting against his brother. and that struggle never stopped. We know he was a schemer and rogue, and that deception was an issue his entire life. He didn't just mess up once or twice, conniving was his lifelong practice. And yet, sinful and deceitful as Jacob was, when he wrestled with God and refused to let Him go until God showed him favor (or grace), that is exactly what God did. In other words, Jacob, a wicked man, a deceiver, came to God and said, "I've done wrong, and the only hope I have is that you will be gracious to me." And what was God's response? Hosea 12:4, "*He* [Jacob] *strove with the angel and prevailed; he wept and sought his favor. He met God at Bethel and there God spoke with us – the Lord, the God of hosts, the Lord is his memorial name.*"

God showed grace and love to a man who did not deserve it at all. And what Hosea was doing here was drawing a parallel between Israel – wicked acts of sin, self-righteous, and rejecting God's authority – and Jacob, a sinner, deceitful in all kinds of ways…and yet God gave grace. God poured out love on both of them even though they did not deserve it. Look at where he does this for Israel in Hosea13:12-13, "*The iniquity of Ephraim is bound up; his sin is kept in store. The pangs of childbirth come for him, but he is an unwise son, for at the right time He does not present himself at the opening of the womb.*" Those verses are describing the sinfulness of Israel, all the reasons why they do not deserve God's love.

But now look at verse 14. "*I shall ransom them from the power of Sheol; I shall redeem them from Death. O, Death, where are your plagues? Oh, Sheol, where is your sting?*" It is interesting to note that those phrases in that verse actually aren't questions in the Hebrew. This is one place where I think the NIV gives a better translation. They aren't questions; they are statements: Death, you have no sting! Does that sound familiar? Paul used that in reference to the resurrection in I Corinthians 15. "Oh grave, where is your victory, Death, where is your sting?"

But here is what God was saying: Your sin is bound up. You deserve wrath, but I'm not going to give it to you. Instead, I shall redeem you from death. Instead, Death won't be victorious over you. Sheol will not sting you. God was promising and pledging the love that He has for His people, just as He did for Jacob, even though none of them deserved it.

The book of Hosea is challenging if you're just reading it through. Hebrew literature, specifically prophetic literature, isn't linear, it is cyclical. Themes cycle around again and again. It is difficult at times. But basically, Hosea shows us all the reasons why Israel did not deserve God's love at all – and why we don't either. The case against us is obvious: the acts of sin, the self-righteousness, the rejection of his authority, over and over. And yet, once again God professes to His people, "I'm not going to dismiss you. I'm not going to get rid of you. I love you. You're mine and I will not forsake you." And the question we *ought* to be asking is, "How can this be?" Because if we're honest with ourselves, it *should not* be this way. So how can this be true?

The Rationale for Being Loved By God

Up until now, the metaphor in the book of Hosea has been the wayward wife, personified by Gomer. The predominant language has been of whoredom, prostitution, spiritual adultery. But in Hosea 11 the metaphor changes and it is no longer the wayward wife; now it is the disobedient son. And this language and metaphor of a child is not unique to the book of Hosea, you see it elsewhere. I'll show you just a couple of examples. Exodus 4:21-22. *"And the Lord said to Moses, 'When you go back to Egypt, see that you do before Pharaoh all the miracles that I have put in your power; but I will harden his heart so that he will not let the people go. Then you shall say to Pharaoh, "Thus says the Lord, **Israel is my firstborn son.**"'"* [Emphasis mine}

Here's another, Jeremiah 31:9, *"With weeping they shall come, and with pleas for mercy I will lead them back, I will make them walk by brooks of water, in a straight path in which they shall not stumble, for **I am a father to Israel and Ephraim is my firstborn.*** [Emphasis mine]

In the latter part of the book of Hosea, and in other places in the Old Testament, Israel is clearly referred to as a son, but we know that in this case, Israel is a prodigal son. Why is this language of a child or firstborn son so significant? Two reasons. The lesser reason is that it proves that Israel is loved because of their birth, not because of their behavior. Israel is loved by their Father because they are His children. God loves His people because they are *His*, good or bad. But the much bigger reason why this new metaphor in Hosea of sonship, of being God's child, is important is because of Hosea 11:1, *"When Israel was a child, I loved him, and out of Egypt I called my son."*

Stay with me here because what I'm about to unpack for you is the absolute, undeniable reality of God's love for you. This is a blessed assurance unlike any you could ever imagine. Israel does not deserve God's love, yet Israel gets God's love, because they're His. *"Out of Egypt I called my son."* Does that sound familiar? Look at Matthew 2:13 and following.

> *"Now when they had departed, behold, an angel of the Lord appeared to Joseph in a dream and said, 'Rise, take the child and his mother and flee to Egypt and remain there until I tell you, for Herod is about to search for the child to destroy him.' And he rose and took the child and his mother by night and departed to Egypt and remained there until the death of Herod. This was to fulfill what the Lord had spoken by the prophet* [Hosea]*, 'Out of Egypt, I called my son.'"*

This was talking about Jesus Christ. And it is referring back to what Hosea wrote hundreds of years before. Now, just a few verses further along we come to this in Matthew 3:16. *"And when Jesus was baptized, immediately he went up from the water, and behold, the heavens were open to him and he saw the Spirit of God descending like a dove and coming to rest on him; and behold, a voice from heaven said, 'This is my beloved son, with whom I am well pleased.'"* Hang with me. We're building to something here, something big. Immediately after His baptism, in Matthew 4:1 we're told, *"Then Jesus was led up by the Spirit into the wilderness to be tempted by the devil. And after fasting forty days and forty nights, he was hungry, and the tempter came and said to him, 'If you are the Son of God, command the stones to become loaves of bread.' But he answered, 'It is written, man shall not live by bread alone, but by every word that comes from the mouth of God.'"* What is this trail through Matthew 2, 3, and 4 clearly teaching us?

Jesus *relived* the story of Israel so that He could *rewrite* the story of Israel.

No part of the life of Jesus was accidental. Every moment of His life had purpose. He relived the story of Israel so that He could rewrite Israel's story. Let's really lay this out:

Israel was called my firstborn son.

Jesus was called the firstborn son.

Israel was brought out of Egypt.

Jesus was brought out of Egypt.

Israel passed through the Red Sea.

Jesus passed through the waters of baptism.

Israel wandered in the wilderness 40 years.

Jesus went into the wilderness for 40 days.

Israel was tempted in the wilderness and failed.

Jesus was tempted in the wilderness and was victorious.

Israel lived by manna in the wilderness.

Jesus, tempted with bread, chose not to live by bread alone, but by the word
  of God.

You see, Israel was the disobedient son. Jesus is the obedient Son in whom the Father is well pleased. Now you may say, "What does that have to do with the love of God for *me*?" Here's what it has to do with you. When you (a repeatedly disobedient child of God) put your faith in Jesus (the perfectly obedient Son), His life of perfect obedience replaces your life of continual disobedience, so that whatever is said of Jesus is said of you, including, "*This is my beloved son in whom I am well pleased.*"

Israel did not deserve the love of God at all. And yet God continually promised His love to this disobedient son. Why? Because the obedient Son took their place. And because He took *our* place, God looks at *you* through the righteousness of Him and says, "I love what I see. You are My Child. You are My Son in whom I am well pleased." Or, as Paul said in Ephesians 1:3, "*Blessed be the God and Father of our Lord Jesus Christ, who has blessed us in Christ with every spiritual blessing in the heavenly places, even as he chose us in him before the foundation of the world, that we should be holy and blameless before him. In love he predestined us for adoption to himself as sons through Jesus Christ, according to the purpose of his will, to the praise of his glorious grace with which he has blessed us in the beloved.*"

When someone puts their faith in Jesus, they are adopted as a son. Through Christ, *you* are adopted by God as His Child, and you have all the rights and privileges and inheritance of the Son of God. Are you ready for the slap? This means that the only way God stops loving *you* is if God stops loving *Jesus.*

You couldn't be more secure.

So thinking—in any way—that God does not love you is blasphemy. Why? Because it denies everything that Jesus did for you in His life and on the cross. He was repeatedly slapped with the reality of your sin. He didn't merely know your sin intellectually, He felt it in His bones and across His flesh, because He loved you. *Through Christ* we are adopted as sons. You are just as disobedient as Israel and you do not deserve the love of God, *yet* (that beautiful word, "yet") God is crazy for you. He's outrageously in love with you, boundlessly in love with you because you are united with the Son in whom God is completely pleased and therefore that is your identity. That is who you are. That's the good news of the gospel. You are loved like the Son of God because you have been united with the Son of God.

Let that sink in, feel the security of that reality because your diagnosis from the Great Physician is not, "You only have a few days to live." Your diagnosis from the Great Physician is, "You're going to live and be loved forever." Forever. You're going to live and you're going to be loved forever because of your union with Jesus. My prayer is that you will experience that existential slap across your face, however many times you need it, until you finally *feel* the love of God and it is no longer just a fact to you, but is something that sets you free.

Twenty

What is He Doing With Her?

As a father of two daughters, I have seen it more than I wanted to. In fact, it was my middle child's favorite *Disney* movie. I am referring to *Beauty and the Beast.* Many of you remember the story. There's a poor inventor who has a daughter by the name of Belle. Most of the villagers see Belle as a little odd because of her love for books, but in spite of that, she is widely admired for her beauty. In fact, there's a man in the village who is absolutely smitten with her. He wants more than anything to marry her. He asks her every day if she will marry him – and he is the kind of guy that every other woman in town wants to marry. His name is Gaston, what a hunk! He is tall and strong and handsome, and without a doubt, he is the best pick in town.

Every guy here'd love to be you, Gaston

Even when taking your lumps.

There's no man in town as admired as you

You're everyone's favorite guy

Everyone's awed and inspired by you

And it's not very hard to see why

No one's slick as Gaston

No one's quick as Gaston

No one's neck's as incredibly thick as Gaston's

For there's no man in town, half as manly

Perfect, a pure paragon!

You can ask any Tom, Dick or Stanley

And they'll tell you whose team they prefer to be on

No one's big like Gaston

A king pin like Gaston

No one's got a swell cleft in his chin like Gaston

(As a specimen, yes, I'm intimidating!)

My what a guy, that Gaston!

I mean, seriously, if Belle has any intelligence, any sense at all, she will marry a guy like that – and that is part of the twist of the whole story. You see, due to a very unfortunate event related to her father, Belle ends up imprisoned by a beast. And while she is imprisoned, much to her shock, she is treated with kindness. In fact, the beast falls in love with her as well, but loving the beast never even occurs to her. After all, how could you love someone who looks like that? I mean, look at him. He's a beast.

Then one day, upon learning that her father is not doing well, Belle asks the beast if she can be released, and he agrees. While Belle is away tending to her father, it dawns on her that she has fallen in love with the beast. And in a shocking turn of events, at least by all worldly standards, Belle ends up marrying, not the pick of the village, a man like Gaston, she ends up marrying the beast. In fact, if you know the story, it is her love that transforms the beast back into a beauty of a man. Yuck.

We all know that Beauty and the Beast is a fairytale. We understand that, but it is also one of the most famous examples in movie and literature and film of an unlikely marriage. I mean, after all, most people would not expect someone as beautiful as a Belle to love someone as beastly as the beast. And yet that often happens in life, does it not? I mean, c'mon, be honest. There are times when you look at a couple and you think, what in the world is he doing with her, or what is she doing with him?

In other words, you take a look at a couple and by all appearances, there doesn't seem to be any rational reason for the two of them to be together. Your assessment may be based on their physical attractions like Beauty and her beast. Maybe it's based on their financial status, maybe it's the fact that they don't seem to have anything in common. Maybe there's a significant age gap between the two. But for whatever the reason, you know that feeling of looking at a couple and saying that's an unlikely pair, that is an unlikely marriage.

And that, in many ways, has been the story in the book of Hosea. I mean, after all, what is Hosea, a prophet of God, a spokesman for God, a man called by God, doing with someone like Gomer, a prostitute, a whore? What is somebody like that doing with someone like her? And of course, if you're mentally overthinking that example, you're missing the point because the real question should be, what is God doing with a people like Israel? Or better yet, what is Jesus doing with me? What is Jesus doing with you? Talk about your odd couple.

Think of it in the book of Hosea. How can the best possible husband in the universe, the God who is forever faithful, love a constantly wayward, consistently unfaithful wife like Israel? I mean every time He makes her prosper, she becomes a prostitute. He never leaves her; she leaves Him time and time again. He wants her; she wants Baal. Seriously, if you were God's relationship counselor (which you are not), you would advise Him to move on. And yet, He remains unshaken in His love for her. Eventually you're just left wondering, what is He doing with her? The reality is that God's love is not based on your "beauty," that is, your good works. God's love is what gives you beauty. It is His love that makes you beautiful. As I've said time and time again in this book, God's love for you is not based on whether you are good or bad. It is based on the fact that you are His. And it is His love that brings your beauty to you.

Now, as we come to the final chapter of this very odd love story in the book of Hosea, we ask, as we do of all love stories, how does it end? And you would think that, by this point, God will finally come to His senses, right? I mean, God, the faithful husband who has been forsaken time and time again by this beastly, sinful bride, will finally get rid of the old hag for good, and go find someone better. Isn't that what you would expect? The wayward wife finally walks away one too many times and the husband calls it quits. How does this love story end?

Hosea 14:1-4, God says, "*Return, O Israel, to the Lord your God, for you have stumbled because of your iniquity. Take with you words and return to the Lord; say to him, 'Take away all iniquity; accept what is good, and we will pay with bulls the vows of our lips. Assyria shall not save us; we will not ride on horses; and we will say no more, "Our God," to the work of our hands. In you the orphan finds mercy.' I will heal their apostasy; I will love them freely, for my anger has turned from them.*" That's how this love story ends.

Notice here the security of God's love. I mean, you've got to admit, this faithful husband that is God is sure consistent. The book of Hosea ends the way it has been throughout, God continually loving His people. Let's break down that last verse. He said, "*I will heal their apostasy.*" Apostasy means a falling away, so He's saying, "Though they have forsaken Me, though they have turned from Me. I will restore them. I will heal them. I will renew the covenant we made together."

Secondly, "*I will love them freely.*" God is saying He doesn't love His people because He has to, because He is obligated. He freely, eagerly loves them. There's no arm twisting here, no deal making, no expectations. It is just free, sovereign, unconditional love that God has for His people. It's crazy. It's absolutely dumbfounding. After all that has been said and done, after everything that Israel has done to their faithful husband, God, He says, "*I'll heal their apostasy. I'll love them freely.*"

And then the third phrase in that verse, "*My anger has turned from them.*" He's not holding a grudge. He's not saying, "I'll love them, but I can't look at their face." It's not. "I will love them, but I'm never going to let 'em forget it." It's not. "I will love them, but they're going to have to sleep on the couch." It's not, "I will love them, but if they do this one more time…" Not at all. After all of Israel's idolatry and spiritual adultery and under-the-table deals with Assyria, this story ends with God saying this, "I will heal them, and I will love them freely, no anger, no grudge." Sounds a lot like what Paul says in 1 Corinthians 13, how "love holds no record of wrongs."

This is not just what the Old Testament book of Hosea says about God and Israel. This is what the New Testament says about Jesus and His bride, *us.* Look at I John 4:10, "*In this is love, not that we have loved God, but that he loved us and sent his son to be the propitiation for our sins.*" You and I did not love God first. He loved us. We were not even able to love Him. Do you remember the old song, Oh, how I love Jesus, Oh, how I love Jesus, Oh, how I love Jesus because he first loved me? The fact is, without God's love, we are unable to love Him, for dead people don't love very well.

The good news of this truth is that His love for you is not conditioned on your love for Him. That is incredible news. God does not love us *because* we loved Him and sought Him out; He sought us out and loved us first. It means that there are no conditions to His love. God simply put His love upon us. He loves you unconditionally, which means God loved you before, God loves you now, and He will love you forever, freely.

But wait, there's more. It gets even better according to Hosea 14:4 and I John 4:10. What this means is the only thing God feels for you is love. The *only* thing He feels for you is *love*. That's it. Hosea put it this way. "*My anger is turned away*." John the Apostle put it this way, "*Jesus is the propitiation for our sins*." Propitiation simply means "the wrath substitute." In other words, all of the righteous anger (and it *is* a righteous anger) that God has towards us and our sin was placed on Jesus Christ at the cross. And that means the only thing He feels for you, even in your present mess, is love. It is the *only* thing He feels for you. It's not 50/50, it's not 90/10, it's not 99.9/0.1, it is 100% love.

It's not love with a little bit of frustration, love with a little bit of hesitation, love with some uncertainty, love with resentment. It is only love. It's not love in the past, but not love in the present. It's not love in the past, and in the present, but not in the future. It is love in the past, love in the now, and love forevermore. That is God's love for you in the person of Jesus Christ. Jesus took God's anger, the righteous anger that our sin deserved. And because Jesus took that wrath, the only thing we receive is God's love. That's how secure that is. Our security for God's love is the person of Jesus Christ.

Twenty One

The reality of God's love really ought to shock you. It ought to be the most shocking news you have ever heard in your life. You should almost be appalled at such a statement. I'm going to try to illustrate this with two pictures. Give me grace, but I'm going to try to give an example to help you feel how shocking this is, that God would love us this way. First we'll go back to Hosea 13:16. It says this about Samaria, which is part of the Northern Kingdom of Israel, "*Samaria shall bear her guilt, because she has rebelled against her God; they shall fall by the sword; their little ones shall be dashed in pieces, and their pregnant women ripped open.*" That's not a verse you find on a coffee mug very often. That's the kind of verse that you probably cringe to find in the Bible. What is that verse about?

That verse is simply God telling Israel what is going to happen when Assyria takes Israel captive in the days to come. There is going to be bloodshed.

There's going to be loss of life. It is going to be brutal. This is prophetic imagery of the judgment that God is warning them about. If they would just repent and turn to Him, He would save them from it. Now, here's my question. Does that bother you? I guarantee you, it bothers a lot of people. If you don't believe me, the next time you're at a Bible study or the next time you're talking to a coworker who is an unbeliever, just read them that verse and make note of their initial reaction. How could God do that? How can God be a God of love and let stuff like that happen? They will be appalled by such a verse.

Now hold that thought and let me give you another picture. I'm not trying to be political. I'm not trying to be cultural. I'm trying to be biblical. As the whole country knows, in 2020, in Minneapolis, a man named George Floyd died in a confrontation with police. The entire country was incensed by that event. But here is my question – and I say this with the purest of hearts – which of the following outcomes would be the most outrageous? The officer charged with the death of George Floyd stands before the judge and receives justice. He gets what he deserves. Or, the officer charged with the death of George Floyd stands before the judge and the judge says this, "All charges are dropped and you're free to go." Which of those two outcomes would you think outrageous?

I'm not giving commentary on one side or the other of that specific event. But I'm pretty sure our culture would have been apoplectic with rage if the officer had walked. We don't have any problem with justice. We demand justice. When it comes to wrongdoing, we cry out for justice (unless, of course, *we* are the sinner). What is almost impossible to think of in relation to sin that is not ours is mercy. Mercy is what is shocking. And while I can't speak to the details relating to the death of George Floyd, I most certainly can speak to the details related to the death of Jesus. Namely, it was *our* sin that nailed him there. You and I are spiritual murderers in the first degree, deserving far more than Assyrian destruction. We deserve eternal damnation. And yet because of Jesus, the verdict over our life is, "I will love you freely and my anger is turned away." That's scandalous. And if you'll honestly stop and think about it, the love of God for sinners, His mercy, is far more outrageous than the judgment of God.

You may ask, why are you saying all this? When we read the last verse of Hosea 13 about the judgment coming upon Israel with the Assyrian captivity, we feel outraged. How *could* God? But then in the next chapter, we read God saying, "I will love you freely," and we think, "Yeah, that sounds about right." We're so ho-hum. It shows just how little we really understand the enormity, the incomprehensibility of God's love for us. There are no words large enough for it. It is simply breathtaking. God's wayward, prodigal people finally return to Him, and when it is all said and done and the love story comes to a close, He says, "I will heal you, and I will love you freely, and there will be no anger for you."

Now, the challenge for us as believers is how do we live in that? How do we live in that love? Once again, I think I John 4:16 is helpful. "*So we have come to know and to believe the love that God has for us. God is love, and whoever abides in love abides in God, and God abides in him.*" Christians are those who not only know God's outrageous boundless love, but we can also come to believe it.

You remember the prodigal son on his way home to the father. He's thinking in his mind, "At best, I'm a slave. There's no way I'm treated like a son. There's no way I *should* be treated like a son. At the very best, I'll be a slave in my father's home." And yet, what Hosea 14 teaches is that not only is God's love for you secure, God's love for you is also *sincere*. You don't have to doubt it. You don't have to question whether or not everything I've written about God's love is true. You're secure. But the security of that love is sincere. God really means it. Let me show you three reasons in Hosea 14 for believing that.

The first thing that I want you to see is God's pleading. Hosea 14:1, *"Return, O Israel, to the Lord your God, for you have stumbled because of your iniquity."* Look at God's plea to Israel, "Return to the Lord, return to the Lord." We've seen God do that repeatedly throughout the book of Hosea. Why does God repeatedly tell his people to come to Him? I'll give you a minute....

It's because He really wants them to come to Him! He is pleading. And the reason He is pleading, "Return home, come back," is because He wants you. And God is not a man that He should lie. He means what He says. You need to stop dwelling on what you think God *should* say and start dwelling on what God *has* said.

The prodigal son thought, "My father's never going to accept me. He probably won't even let me through the front door." And where, actually, was the prodigal's father? Outside, staring at the horizon hoping to see his son coming home to him! Have we not been surprised over and over during this study of Hosea when God said He would forgive, He would heal, He would love? That surprise means we need another existential slap, because we still don't *know* in our bones that all He feels for us is *love*. When we finally come to believe that, like the Apostle John said, we will abide in that love and no longer question it.

In this unlikely marriage that is the Church and Jesus, I'm quite certain that He is the rational one. And I'm quite certain that He is the one that speaks the truth. So, in black and white letters, God is saying to His people, "I want you to come home. Come home." Believe Him when He calls you home.

A second thing that shows the sincerity of God's love is His pattern. I take this from Hosea 14:2-3, *"Take with you words and return to the Lord; say to him, 'Take away all iniquity; accept what is good, and we will pay with bulls the vows of our lips. Assyria shall not save us; we will not ride on horses; we will say no more, "Our God," to the work of our hands. In you the orphan finds mercy."* I won't take the time to break down every little phrase in these two verses, but here's a basic summary of what those verses are saying: If you go to God with words of praise on your lips, acknowledging your idolatry, just like an orphan, you receive mercy every time.

God has a pattern of showing mercy. At this point in Old Testament history, God can say, "I'm pretty sure I've got a resume that is impeccable when it comes to showing you mercy. I have received you back time and time again." The problem is that you and I are like orphans, we've gotten so used to rejection that it's hard for us to really believe that we *will* be accepted. We forget the pattern of mercy that God has shown us.

Ernie Johnson is a broadcaster for TNT and covers the NBA. He and his wife, Cheryl, have adopted several children. Two of their older children, Ashley and Allison, were adopted from the foster care system. Now, Ashlyn and Allison were bounced around for quite a bit during their earlier life. They had learning disabilities, they had been abused at times, and Ernie said that, "One of the biggest hurdles when they first came into the family was getting them to accept that we were not going to send them back." He described the moment when he really saw this during a conversation between Allison and his wife. Cheryl had just finished explaining to Allison, "This is your forever home." And Allison looked at Cheryl and said, "Well, how long will forever be this time?" You see the pattern of their life had been rejection – You're not loved, you're not accepted – so it was hard for them to comprehend that this could actually be a forever home.

God has a pattern throughout all of redemptive history of showing mercy to those who come to Him with a genuine heart. So if you doubt how sincere God's love is for you, look at His regular pleading, "Come home. Come home." He doesn't just say that to say it, He means it. And look at His pattern. Time and time and time again He has shown you the grace and love that you do not deserve.

There's a third reason why we can know that God's love is sincere. In Hosea 14:5-7, I want you to notice God's passion. *"I will be like the dew to Israel; he shall blossom like the lily; he shall take root like the trees of Lebanon; his shoots shall spread out; his beauty shall be like the olive, and his fragrance like Lebanon. They shall return and dwell underneath my shadow; they shall flourish like the grain; they shall blossom like the vine; their fame shall be like the wine of Lebanon."* Let's be honest, that kind of language does not mean much to us. I mean, we read that and we think, "Okay, that sounds nice." What in the world does it mean? Do you have any idea where that language comes from? Bible trivia here: That is the language of the song of Solomon, God's book of romance and passionate love in the Old Testament. It is actually much like Hosea and Gomer, a symbol of God's passionate love for His bride, for His people.

Even our modern sensibilities can see the romantic overtones of "blossom like a flower," "beauty like an olive," "fragrance like Lebanon," and especially "dwell underneath my shadow," an image of drawing someone in closely. It is the same language. It is also the same language that God used back in Hosea 2 when God said, "*I will allure her, I will speak tenderly to her.*" So, what is God doing? How does this love story end? It ends with love, passionate love. And if that throws you off, if you think it's weird to talk about it that way, here's what you need to understand. God's love for you is so intimate. It is so intimate that the closest human expression that we can even relate it to is romantic passion. The best we can do, humanly speaking, is to use that kind of metaphor, that kind of illustration.

Still, the unlikely love story of God and Israel, Beauty and the Beast, doesn't have a Disney ending – yet. But the book of Hosea ends with God telling His people, "Come home to me. I will heal you and love you freely. I've shown you a pattern of mercy time and time again, because I have a passion for you, an intimate passion for my bride. I truly, sincerely love you," a declaration of God's desire for His wayward wife. It is deeply moving. And absolutely lovely.

Another very unlikely marriage is the one between Jesus and you as a part of His bride. I mean, seriously, who would have ever put the two of you together? And the answer to that question, of course, is God. God put you together. That's not a joke. It's not a misprint in your Bible. It is the sincere love of God for you and the person of Jesus Christ. And so sincere is that love that God sent His only son as a propitiation for our sins. The good news of the gospel is that the Beauty became the beast to make the beast beautiful forever.

And because of that, the only thing God feels for you is love. And that is how your love story ends.

Twenty Two

Philip Blanks caught hundreds of passes as a wide receiver, but not one of them compared to the grab he made a few years ago. Blanks played wide receiver in high school for Kalamazoo High School in Michigan. He went on to play wide receiver in football at Saddleback College in California. Blanks was also a retired US Marine and it was that training on the football field and that training in the service that prepared him for this life saving moment.

Blanks was visiting a friend in Phoenix, Arizona. He and his friend decided that they would take a walk to the local barbershop, and as they did, they walked past an apartment building that had caught on fire. They could hear cries for help, so they rushed to the building to see what they could do. As they arrived, they heard a woman screaming on a third-floor balcony. She was holding a small child over the rail, preparing to throw him to someone below to save him from the flames that were already engulfing her. That was when Blanks took action, racing over to catch that little boy and save his life.

As you can imagine, Blanks was interviewed by a host of different media outlets. At one interview he said this, "It all happened so fast, it was a blur. I started running and all I saw was a baby. But the boy's mother is the real hero. She was the one who was willing to make the ultimate sacrifice to save her child."

Stories like that are inspiring. Stories of rescue, stories where lives are saved, stories about heroic people who sacrifice themselves to save others. And we see stories like that all the time. We see headlines like this: 14-year-old Boy Saves Four Men From Drowning, or Woman's Smartwatch Saves Her Life, or Dog Saves Freezing Man, or Man Saves Girl From Shark Attack. We see stories of salvation, stories of rescue all the time. And not only do we see and hear such stories, but we use that same kind of language in everyday conversation. For instance, you might say or hear, their marriage was saved, his job was saved, the baby was saved.

When we see stories like Philip Blank's, or when we use that salvation kind of language in everyday conversation, we almost always mean survived, rescued from certain death, kept from danger. Take the examples that I just gave you. If someone were to say their marriage was saved, what is meant by that is that the marriage didn't end in divorce. Or if we say that his job was saved, what we mean is that, though there was a series of layoffs, his job wasn't cut. If we say the baby was saved, we mean that something went wrong with the pregnancy, but the baby survived. We usually think of salvation as surviving, just squeaking by, avoiding by a hair.

And, of course, the same thing is true spiritually or biblically. We say things like, "I'm saved," or "God saved me," or "Jesus saves." And what do we usually mean by that? Well, we mean, I'm not going to Hell. I won't have to face the wrath of God. I won't be defeated by death. I'm saved from my sins. In short, surviving. Now, don't get me wrong. I'm not suggesting that that isn't true because it certainly is true. But it's incomplete. It is wholly true, but it is not the whole truth. It's not a full understanding of God's saving love.

Salvation is so much more than merely surviving. Salvation is *thriving*. We are not just saved *from* something, we are saved *to* something. Let me give you some human examples, it's not just being saved from the shark attack, it's being saved to a seaside resort where you're able to write the book you always wanted to write. It's not just that you're saved from the burning apartment building, but you're saved to an Upper West Side apartment where you can enjoy the skyline of Manhattan. Biblically speaking, you're not just saved from God's judgment; you are saved *to* God's love. You are saved from a life separated from God to a life where you can enjoy God. You are saved from certain death to abundant life. And that is exactly what I want to show you here in the last two chapters of Hosea.

Hosea 13:15 says, "*Though he may flourish among his brothers, the east wind, the wind of the Lord, shall come, rising from the wilderness, and his fountain shall dry up; his spring shall be parched; it shall strip his treasury of every precious thing. Samaria shall bear her guilt because she is rebelled against her God. They shall fall by the sword; their little ones shall be dashed in pieces, and their pregnant women ripped open.*" Of course, these are not verses that we want to read. As I've explained earlier, these are verses that speak to the Assyrian captivity that is soon to come upon the Kingdom of Israel in Hosea's time.

Remember that Jewish literature uses a lot of metaphor. Here God is using the wind to describe the coming judgment. Though Israel has flourished under His care even while they were unfaithful, the wind of God's judgment is going to come. God warns them that the wind will dry up their fountain, their spring shall be parched – there is going to be famine. Then God gets quite literal, very specific: They will fall by the sword. There is going to be military conquest and even their women and children will be brutally murdered by Assyria.

Israel knew that this was no hyperbole. This was how Assyria did war. They operated on a policy of sheer, unadulterated terror. In fact, they published their atrocities in stone. Here is an inscription found on a temple in the city of Nimrod describing what King Ashurbanipal did to the leaders of Suru: "I built a pillar at the city gate and I flayed [skinned while alive] all the chief men who had revolted and I covered the pillar with their skins; some I walled up inside the pillar, some I impaled upon the pillar on stakes." So when Hosea described what was to come if they did not repent, it was not discounted as, "too bad to be true;" it was Assyria's reputation.

Another prophet in the Old Testament, Nahum, gives an eyewitness account of what happened when Assyria did, indeed, fall upon the Northern Kingdom. This is Nahum 3:1-3:

"Woe to the bloody city, all full of lies and plunder – no end to the prey! The crack of the whip, and rumble of the wheel, galloping horse and bounding

chariot! Horsemen charging, a flashing sword and glittering spear, host of slain, heaps of corpses, dead bodies without end – they stumble over the bodies!"

That's a description of the situation that Israel is about to be in when the Assyrian captivity comes upon them in 721-722 BC. But what God was saying here is that, "I'm going to take you from a place like that to a very different scenario." Now look at chapter 14:4. It says, "*I will heal their apostasy; I will love them freely, for my anger has turned from them. I will be like the dew to Israel; he shall blossom like the lily; he shall take root like the trees of Lebanon; his shoots shall spread out; his beauty shall be like the olive, and his fragrance like Lebanon. They shall return and dwell beneath my shadow; they shall flourish like the grain; they shall blossom like the vine; their fame shall be like the wine of Lebanon.*"

In other words, God is going to save Israel, but not just from the atrocities described in Hosea 13. Here's a quick summary of the verses that we just read, God is going to save them to a place of:

Restoration, for they will blossom like a flower, in a place of Strength that is like the trees of Lebanon, those big cedar trees. A place of Prosperity, where they will be fruitful like the olive tree, in a place that's Pleasant, like the fragrance of Lebanon, a place of Flourishing, for there'll be grain in the field, fruit on the vine, a place of Reputation, for they will have fame like the wine of Lebanon.

All of those descriptions, to the mind of one living in the ancient near east, are descriptions of prosperity.

A Salvation of Prosperity

Here is the first point that I want to show you. God is going to save Israel, not just *from* something awful, but *to* something that is very, very beautiful. She is not simply being brought back to neutral. God is not simply trying to maintain a covenant, but to renew communion. It's not just that He wants to bring you back into some neutral relationship He wants to bring you back into *flourishing*. God's saving love towards His people is not merely a matter of surviving; it is thriving. Which is, frankly, hard to believe. Think about it, after all the unfaithfulness of the people of Israel, after all of her idolatry and spiritual adultery, the thing God wants for His people is not just their survival but their prosperity. That's amazing.

So let me say this, though it might make you very uncomfortable. The gospel is a prosperity gospel. Let me clarify what I mean. When I say that the gospel is a prosperity gospel, I do not mean the health and wealth prosperity gospel that has become so common and popular in America. It's not the one where you use Jesus to get a new car, you use Jesus to never get sick, you use Jesus so that every day can be a Friday, you use Jesus to "name it and claim it." That teaching is nonsense and contrary to the true gospel. But just because the gospel is not *that* kind of prosperity gospel does not mean that the gospel is not a prosperity gospel. You see, God wants flourishing and prosperity for his people.

How do they get it?

The Source of Prosperity

This is huge. This is significant. In fact, this is what separates the true prosperity gospel from the false prosperity gospel that we hear so much of today. Look at Hosea 14:5, and 8, "*I will be like the dew to Israel; and he shall blossom like the lily; he shall take root like the trees of Lebanon.*" And now verse eight, "*O, Ephraim, what have I to do with idols? It is I who answer and look after you. I am like an evergreen cypress; from me comes your fruit.*" In other words, what is the source of this prosperity? In verse five, "I will be like the dew to Israel." That is the water source from which all of this flourishing will come, all of this prosperity, all of this blossoming is from God. Or in verse eight, where does the fruitfulness come from? God says, "*From me.*" The source of all of this promised prosperity is God Himself.

God is taking his wayward people from a place of judgment to a place of passion and prosperity – by saving His people to Himself. God loves you so much that even though you have repeatedly turned from Him, He wants to save you. But He doesn't just want to save you from Hell. He wants to save you to Himself. He doesn't just want to save you from destruction. He wants to save you to delight. He doesn't just want to save you from punishment. He wants to save you to prosperity. He doesn't just want to save you from death. He wants to save you to everlasting life.

Or, to use the metaphor of the book of Hosea, God wants to save his adulterous wife, not just by bringing her back into the house or just getting her off of the street. He wants to save her back into the bedroom, because He doesn't merely want us saved from our idols, He wants us saved to intimacy with Him. God doesn't just want you to survive, God wants you to thrive. He loves you so much. He wants your life to be a life of prosperity.

But what is the substance of that prosperity? Is it getting a new car? Is it getting more money in the bank? No, it's getting Him. It is the fountain of forever joy. The fountain of living waters. God is saving his people unto Himself. And this is the difference between the false prosperity gospel and the true prosperity gospel.

The false prosperity gospel views Jesus as a way to *get* treasure.

The real prosperity gospel views *Jesus* as the treasure.

The Substitutes For Prosperity

Look at what God says in Hosea 14:8, "*O Ephraim, what have I to do with idols? It is I who answer and look after you.*" What do I have to do with idols? What do idols have to do with Me? I am the one who takes care of you. I am the one who looks out for you. I am the one who makes your life prosperous. Think about it. What makes false gods "false" gods is they make false promises that only the true God can make. What lie does a false god make? The promise that it will make you prosper. The promise that it will make you flourish.

The promise goes like this: If I have __fill in the blank__ (if I have him/her, if I have that thing, if I have that lifestyle), then my life will prosper, then my life will flourish, then my life will blossom like the flower. If I have that perfect spouse, if I have that perfect job, if I can have that physical appearance, I'll flourish. But instead of giving you prosperity, your idol slowly destroys your life.

Let me show you the progression of idolatry, the way it works. It starts with a promise. I'll use the example of money, the love of money.

> *The Promise: So money will say, "If you will worship me, if you make me the god of your life, I'll make your life secure." That is the promise that that idol gives.*
>
> *The Sacrifice: Now you have to sacrifice to it. So, you work harder, you work longer hours, you sacrifice the rest that you need, you sacrifice time with family, etc.*
>
> *Fulfillment: You get the raise, you get more money, you "prosper."*
>
> *Disillusionment: You realize it's not what you thought it would be. It's not enough.*
>
> *Intensification: You double down. You work harder, longer, you sacrifice more until:*
>
> *Destruction: You realize you have sacrificed everything that matters for a god that is never enough.*

There is an alternative progression in which you accept the promise, make the sacrifice, and then, rather than getting fulfillment, you end up in failure. That is, you don't get the raise, you don't get more money, and you feel like a failure. What happens then is you run to a *different* idol. You realize the idol of money didn't work, so maybe the idol of love will. The idol of love didn't work, so maybe the idol of accomplishments will work. You keep chasing after all these idols that are promising you what only God can give you. That is why they are false gods. (I suppose they'd be true gods if they promised death and destruction, but then they wouldn't have any worshippers, would they?)

So, the entire time you're seeking prosperity, you are actually running from the true source of prosperity, the one that can actually make your life fruitful and meaningful and full of purpose. Here is the difference between the true God and these false gods.

False gods make *you* sacrifice for *them*.

The true God has already sacrificed for *you*.

Twenty Three

The Stability of Prosperity

God takes His people of Israel from something awful to something beautiful, to a prosperous life, but that prosperous life is found in Him, not in Baal. And if they would learn that, and if you and I would learn that, then our life would begin to be stable.

Look at Hosea 14:9, *"Whoever is wise, let him understand these things. Whoever is discerning, let him know them; for the ways of the Lord are right, and the upright walk in them, but transgressors stumble in them."* The book ends with, "Here's how you get the stable life, the life that doesn't stumble." Israel has stumbled time and time and time again throughout this book. So God says here at the closing of the book, "Let the wise understand these things so that you're not stumbling around everywhere." So your life can have a sense of peace to it, so that your soul can rest, so contentment can settle in. Then what happens is that you start to live in His love, you don't have to chase after Baal. You don't have to chase after all those other substitutes. You can just rest in the fact that you are loved by God, and experience a life that is thriving, that is prosperous.

You may be thinking, "Thriving? Have you paid attention to the news lately? Life is anything but thriving right now. I mean, look around. Look at the economy. Look at the situation that we're seeing in our culture. Look at my life. Look at what I'm going through. How can you say thriving?"

How was the Apostle Paul able to thrive in a prison cell? How was the early church in the book of Acts able to thrive as they were facing real persecution? The answer is simply, when our prosperity is in Christ and not our circumstances, we are always thriving. And that is why Christians, more than anybody else in the world, ought to be thriving right now, even in the midst of difficult times. Why? Because we have the ultimate eternal treasure, the ultimate prosperity of life, and His name is Jesus Christ.

When it comes to the saving love of God, it is not just about your surviving, being rescued from the burning building of Hell, being snatched just in the nick of time from the sting of death. No, no. It *is* that, but it is so much more. Instead, it is God's saving love, *plus* bringing you to a place of thriving. And Jesus said this in John 10:9-10, "*I am the door. If anyone enters by me, he will be saved and he will go in and out and find pasture. The thief comes to steal and kill and destroy. I came that they may have life and have it more abundantly.*"

After all, it was Jesus Himself, the author of our salvation, who did not merely survive the cross, but three days later thrived over death and the grave .

He thrived. And that is the outrageous love of God for you in the person of Jesus Christ.

Twenty Four

The Wisdom of Hosea

At the 89th Academy Awards, it stole the show. This film won six Academy Awards, including best director, best actress, best cinematography, best original score, best original song and best production design. In addition to winning the six awards, it received a total of fourteen nominations that tied the record for the most nominations by a single film. The movie that I'm referring to is the movie called *La La Land*. It's a movie about a couple that meets in Hollywood. Maya, played by Emma Stone, is a struggling actress who has dropped out of college and moves to Hollywood from her small town in Nevada. She's trying to pursue her lifelong dream of being an actress on the big screen and it is there in Hollywood that she meets Sebastian.

Sebastian is a jazz pianist who loves traditional jazz music and wants to preserve that tradition, so his intention is to open up his own jazz club. Both Maya and Sebastian are passionate, driven people and that's why they hit it off so well. It's why they almost immediately fall in love. They inspire one another, they see one another through many obstacles, they provide each other the kind of energy they need to endure, and it's obvious, it is just *so* obvious, that they are meant to be together. Then, in the closing scene, Sebastian is playing the piano in his jazz club. As he is playing, Maya pictures their future in her mind, marriage, pregnancy, parenthood, the passage of years together, and all the kinds of things that they would experience together, and it's so sweet, it's going to be beautiful. She gets up and walks to the door where she turns to look back at him sitting there on the piano bench. They share a long look as though they are alone in the room; they exchange a smile; he nods his head.

And then she exits, and he turns to the band, "1, 2, a-1-2-3-4" – and that's it. Wait, what? They don't end up together? She's leaving? Hold on. The movie's not supposed to end like that. This isn't how it's supposed to be. I mean, they're perfect for one another, they're *meant* to be together – I thought they'd live happily ever after. I mean, isn't that how love stories are supposed to end?

Have you ever had that feeling? Have you ever been so sure about an expected outcome and then been completely shocked by a different one? Haven't you experienced a relationship that didn't end the way it should have, a game that didn't end the way everyone thought it would, a journey that ended up in a completely unexpected place, a loved life that was cut short? I'm quite sure you have. We all know that feeling of saying, wait a minute, that's not the right ending. That's exactly the way we feel when we get to the end of the book of Hosea. And here's what I mean by that. This great Old Testament love story is supposed to end on the final note of the song with happily ever after. But instead, it ends like this, "*Whoever is wise, let him understand these things; whoever is discerning, let him know them; for the ways of the Lord are right, and the upright walk in them, but transgressors stumble in them.*"

If you've been following along with the book at all, you may be thinking, "Wait a minute, that's not the ending of a great love story." And that's not how this great love story of Hosea and Gomer, and God and Israel is supposed to end. Maybe the book should have just stopped. Look at Hosea 14:4, it says, "*I will heal their apostasy; I will love them freely, for my anger has turned from them.*" Now, that's more like it. That's a happily-ever-after ending to a love story. We might think that's how the book is supposed to end, but it doesn't. The final scene in the movie, the final note in the song, the final verse in the book doesn't end the way one would expect. In fact, what happens in this final verse is that it jumps genre.

We've been following along with the genre of prophecy and, all of a sudden, the book ends with wisdom. It is prophetic genre the whole way through, and then the final note of the song is like something out of the book of Proverbs. In fact, Hosea ends in a way that *no other* Old Testament prophetic book ends. It follows the normal pattern of prophetic literature: An indictment against Israel, the verdict that comes from God, the warning of judgment, and then the promise of restoration. This is exactly what we see in all of the other prophets. It follows the proper structure and the proper pattern of a prophetic book. And then this verse. Full stop. The reader is left to think, "Wait a minute. That's not the ending I expected."

Imagine you've been watching a dramatic thriller full of tragedy, suspense, and on-the-edge-of-your-seat intensity, and then you get to the very final scene and they tell a joke – with a pratfall. You're like, "Wha—? Wait a minute, I thought I was watching *this*, and you end it like *that*? That's what the book of Hosea does. Notice the language again, "*Whoever is wise, let him understand these things; whoever is discerning, let him know them; for the ways of the Lord are right, and the upright walk in them, but transgressors stumble in them.*" Look at that language: "Wise," "discerning," "understanding the ways of the Lord," "the upright," "transgressors stumble." Go read Psalm 1 or Proverbs 10 and you'll think Hosea 14:9 looks much more like wisdom literature than it does prophetic literature. "The upright," for instance, is mentioned around 50 times in the book of Proverbs.

So what's going on here? Because when this kind of shift at the end takes place, it ought to grab our attention. We should be asking why. What is the author trying to do? And here is the answer. The reason why it ends with wisdom is because Hosea, the author, is asking the reader to go back and look at the book *practically*, just as you're meant to do with Proverbs. Proverbs are about everyday life. They're about practical living: decisions that you make, how you spend your money, the way you talk, whether you're a hard worker or lazy. It is all about practical life. And so what Hosea is doing beautifully, and inspired by God, is telling us to go back and look at all the things that we've learned in the book as practical wisdom. And what practical lesson has Hosea been trying to teach us? If we distill the book of Hosea down to a pithy proverb, what will that proverb be?

The one who loves the Lord lives the good life,

for what you love determines how you live.

That is my best effort at the Hosea proverb. It is the wise saying, the practical advice of the book of Hosea. Let me prove it to you. Let me take some time to unpack that proverb phrase by phrase.

The One Who Loves the Lord

The primary issue that God had with the people of Israel in the book of Hosea was their lack of love for Him. That was the fundamental issue, the primary indictment against them. The essential issue God had was that they did not love Him. Let me give you a few examples of that.

Hosea 4:1, *"Hear the word of the Lord, O, children of Israel, for the Lord has a controversy with the inhabitants of the land. There is no faithfulness or steadfast love, and no knowledge of God in the land."*

Hosea 6:4, *"What shall I do with you, O Ephraim? What shall I do with you, O Judah? Your love is like a morning cloud, like the dew that goes early away."*

Hosea 6:6, *"For I desire steadfast love and not sacrifice."*

In other words, it is clear to see that the issue God has with Israel is that they do not love Him. And that is, after all, the first and most important commandment – to love God. They had entered into a covenant with God where they would love Him and obey Him, and they have not. They stood there at Mount Sinai in that marriage ceremony, that covenant ceremony, and they said, *"All that you have said, we will do."* And yet they were unfaithful even before the words were inscribed. As we have seen in the book of Hosea, and in all of Israel's books of history, they turned to other lovers. So the proverb is put positively as "The one who loves the Lord." That is what God wants. He wants you to love Him.

Lives the Good Life

The Book of Proverbs is all about living the good life. Now, you can describe that in different ways. You can say the good life, or the beautiful life, or as we see in Hosea 14:9, the stable life. But it is all the *blessed* life, and it comes when you love God. Now, let me show you that from the book of Hosea.

Hosea 14:1. *"Return, O Israel, to the Lord your God, for you have stumbled because of your iniquity,"* God begins by saying. "Come to me, return to me," that is, "Love me again. Come back to your first love."

Hosea 14:4, *"I will heal their apostasy; I will love them freely, for my anger has turned from them."* You return to Me, and you are healed, you are restored, you are made whole. You are brought back to a healthy place.

Hosea 14:5 , *"I'll be like the dew to Israel. He shall blossom like the lily; he shall take root like the trees of Lebanon; his shoots shall spread out; his beauty shall be like the olive, and his fragrance like Lebanon. They shall return and dwell underneath my shadow; they shall flourish like the grain; they shall blossom like the vine; their fame shall be like the wine of Lebanon."* Talk about the good life. This is flourishing. You will have a prosperous life in God. You will have a beautiful life.

Hosea 14:9, *"...For the ways of the Lord are right, and the upright walk in them, but transgressors stumble in them."* You won't stumble. That is, you will have a stable life.

The point is that the one who loves God, the one who comes to God and loves Him as their First Love, lives the good life, they experience the blessed life that is only found in God. Or you might put it this way: The good life is the God life. I believe the wisdom of Hosea is that those who love the Lord live the good life. The whole book is about loving God. And when you love God, as you see in chapter 14, and in other places, life is prosperous, it flourishes.

For What You Love Determines How You Live

This, too, is taught throughout the book of Hosea. How you think and speak and behave is related to what you love. Let me show you an example of this.

Hosea 4:16, *"Like a stubborn heifer, Israel is stubborn. Can the Lord now feed them like a lamb in a broad pasture?* You may think that's a really odd verse to read. What point does that prove? Let me ask you this, why was Israel called a *heifer*, specifically? Do you remember whom they were worshiping? Baal. And do you remember the image that represented Baal? It was a cow. In other words, Israel had become like what they worshiped. Israel had become like their idol. That thing that they loved more than God influenced the way that they lived, impacted the life they had.

Psalm 115:4, *Their idols are silver and gold, The work of human hands. They have mouths, but do not speak; eyes, but do not see. They have ears, but do not hear; noses, but do not smell. They have hands, but do not feel; feet, but do not walk; and they do not make a sound in their throat. **Those who make them become like them**; so do all who trust in them.*" [Emphasis mine] You become like what you love.

And, of course, you know this in a very practical way. For instance, if you are in love with someone, you begin to do things that they like to do. If you love your kids, you begin to like the things that they like. If you love a group or really want acceptance in a particular group, you begin to adapt your behavior in order to fit in with that group.

Consider your behavior if you have a favorite sports team. You may buy their merchandise, like a jersey or hat or license plate. You may spend money to go to a game. You may restructure your TV package or streaming service to make sure that you can get the game. You may adjust your schedule to make sure that you can watch it when it's on. You're sad when they lose. You're happy when they win. You talk about the game with others. You have opinions about what plays were run. Here's my point, in this simple example alone, your love for that team has determined the clothing you wear, the way you spend your time and money, whether you're in a good mood or a bad mood, the kinds of conversation you have, perhaps even your choice of friends. And that's all because you love a sports team. How much more a truly significant lover? My point is you adapt the way you live to what you love. And even more the things that we really cherish.

You will resemble what you revere. You will conform to what you cherish. It will impact your life. And there may be no greater example of this than the character Gollum in the Lord of the Rings. Let me read just an excerpt of the Lord of the Rings referring to Gollum's obsession with the ring. Here's what Tolkien writes.

> *At the bottom of the tunnel, a cold lake far from the light. And on an island rock in the water lived Gollum. He was a loathsome little creature. He paddled in a small boat with his large flat feet, peering with pale, luminous eyes, and catching blind fish with his long fingers and eating them raw. He ate any living thing if he could possibly catch it and strangle it without a struggle. He possessed a secret treasure that had come to him years ago when he still lived in the light, a ring of gold that made its wearer invisible. It was the one thing he loved, his Precious, and he talked to it even when it was not with him.*

He was so obsessed with the ring, he was so in love with the ring that it changed everything about his life. In fact, even physically in the movie, you see that Gollum goes from looking like a human to looking like some sort of amphibian. His idolatry impacted him. In fact, idolatry makes you subhuman. Here's why. Humanity was created in the image of God to love God, to find its source and fulfillment in God. So when your ultimate love is something other than God, you, like Gollum, become subhuman. You drift from true humanity to sub-humanity because your source of identity is no longer God, and you begin to pattern yourself after something else.

So what is the proverb of Hosea? What's the wisdom that it is trying to teach? I believe it is this, *The one who loves the Lord lives the good life – they prosper, they flourish – for what you love determines how you live.* Love God and you get the good life because the thing that you love is going to impact the way you live. Or, of course, the flip side of that would be, the one who loves something(s) other than God won't live the good life. You'll live a subhuman life, you'll live a less prosperous life because you're loving something other than God. So there you go. Go love the Lord and live the good life....

Twenty Five

Imagine if the book ended there, with a command to "Go live the good life." To just "Love God better." I hope you see the problem with this, namely, none of us can love God that way on our own. In fact, if the book of Hosea proves anything at all, it proves the fact that we do not love God the way we should. It reveals how frequently we fall short of loving God. We aren't any different from Israel, and throughout the book of Hosea, even though Israel had said, "I do," Israel repeatedly did *not*.

You remember the two primary metaphors in the book of Hosea that were used to represent Israel. The first was a wayward wife, a whoring wife. Look at Hosea 2:19. "*I will betroth you to me forever. I will betroth you to me in righteousness and in justice, in steadfast love and in mercy. I will betroth you to me in faithfulness. And you shall know the Lord.*" That is, you are married to God. You are God's bride. We know, of course, from the New Testament, that we are the bride of Christ. We have entered into covenant with Jesus. You are His wife. But do you know what kind of wife you are? A whore. And I'm not trying to be provocative. *God* is trying to be provocative. I'm just communicating the very language that the book of Hosea uses. We are a wife to Jesus. We are the bride of Christ, but the kind of bride we are is a whore.

We've looked at this many times. Hosea 2:2, *"Plead with your mother, plead – for she is not my wife, and I'm not her husband – that she put away her whoring from her face, and her adultery from between her breasts."* And look at Hosea 2:13. *"I will punish her for the feast days of the Baals when she burned offerings to them and adorned herself with her ring and jewelry, and went after her lovers and forgot me, declares the Lord."* Israel's history proves that she is an unfaithful wife, Gomer's adultery in the book of Hosea is the metaphor of idolatry. Just like God told Hosea to go marry a prostitute and have children with a prostitute while she continued to prostitute herself, in the same way God married Israel knowing full well the whoring she would do, knowing full well the idolatry she would involve herself in. And *who* would intentionally marry a whore?

God would marry a whore. And God did.

Think about it this way, "For while we were yet sinners, Christ died for us." Jesus died for us, not after we got our act together, not once we cleaned up our lives. He died for us while we were still a mess; while we were still in our sin, He loved us.

The second metaphor in the book of Hosea was a rebellious son. In Hosea 11:1, God says, "When Israel was a child, I loved him, and out of Egypt I called my son. The more they were called, the more they went away; they kept sacrificing to the Baals and burning offerings to the idols." In other words, in addition to being a wayward wife, Israel was the Old Testament version of the prodigal son, constantly running to other gods.

But God never stopped loving His rebellious child, never stopped loving His wayward son. Here is what He says in Hosea 11:8, *"How can I give you up, O Ephraim? How can I hand you over, O Israel? How can I make you like Admah? How can I treat you like Zeboiim? My heart recoils within me; my compassion grows warm and tender."* God can't help but love His children. He will not let them go, though they have turned from Him many times, Again, God loves you, not because you're good or bad; He loves you because you are His.

And as parents, we know this on a smaller level, right? I mean, why do you go to that fifth-grade school band concert? Is it because you love out-of-tune, glass-shattering, poorly produced concerts? Of course not. Is it because you love fifth graders? Of course not. It is because you love a particular fifth grader. There is a fifth grader that you have set your heart on and that you love more than anything. And if that is true of you, being sinful, how much more is that true for your heavenly Father who is perfect? Don't you see? He adores you. He loves you because you are His. And that's why He never gives up on you.

And why is God able to love you this way? It is because when you, as a repeatedly disobedient child, put your faith in Jesus, the perfectly obedient son, His life of obedience becomes your life of obedience. So whatever is said of Jesus is said of you, including, *"This is my son in whom I am well pleased."* Unless you're prepared to say that God doesn't love Jesus, you can never say that God doesn't love you. What matters is not how you think God should feel about you, but how God *actually* feels about you.

The proverb of Hosea is, The one who loves the Lord lives the good life because what you love determines how you live. That is clearly the teaching of the book of Hosea. The problem is we don't love God that way, certainly not on our own. Even if we determine, "I'm going to love God with all my heart," we, like Israel, will fail time and time and time again. Yet what we have seen is God's unrelenting, boundless, unconditional love towards you.

Let me ask you, after reading again and again about God's outrageous love for you, how do you feel towards God now? What has that done in your relationship with God? If the truth of God's love has actually started to sink in, then what's happening is that your heart has started to warm for God. It has started to stir up your affections for God. It has increased your desire for God. And that is the practicality of the book of Hosea.

What do I mean? If the proverb of Hosea is this, The one who loves the Lord lives the good life for your life is determined by the one you love – and I believe it is – if that is true, and yet we are entirely unable, in and of ourselves, to live up to that proverb, just like Israel was (and after all, our history proves this), then what should you do? What should your response be? Here it is: You should rest daily in God's love for you. You should rest daily in God's unchanging and boundless love for you. You need to be convinced every day that God loves you. You need to be believe Romans 8, that there is nothing at all that can separate you from the love of God. Why? Because as you remain in His love, as you believe His love, as you accept the reality of His love, you naturally start to love God, and in return, live the beautiful life. As you rest in

His love and accept the reality of His love, you begin to naturally love God back. How could you not? You were *created* to love Him. It is a simple, stunning, cycle: *Rest in God's love for you, Rekindle your love for God, Resulting in a good life.*

That is the practical wisdom of the book of Hosea. You don't need Five Steps to the Love of God, or Five Creative Ways to Love God More. That's not wisdom. Here is wisdom: Rest in God's boundless love for you because as you do, you'll love Him more. His love will rekindle yours for Him. And the result of that will be the prosperous life, the beautiful life, the good life.

Have you ever experienced the feeling that something ended in the way it wasn't supposed to? The story ended in a different way than you expected? If you're a follower of Jesus Christ, if you're a Christian, if you're a child of God, you most certainly know that feeling because that is your story. Your story, like Israel's, was that of a wayward wife. Your story, like Israel's, was that of a rebellious child. And yet your love story will not end the way it should end, with separation from God. Your story is going to end with the boundless eternal love of God for you in Christ Jesus. All because Jesus took the ending that you *should* have received, so that He could give you a life of happily ever after.

That is the good news of the Gospel in Hosea!

---

[1] Also translated as "mercy" in many versions.